Becoming
Street
Smart

Becoming Street Smart

Frank MacHovec

NEW
HORIZON
PRESS

Far Hills,
New Jersey

Requests for permission should be addressed to:
New Horizon Press
P.O. Box 669
Far Hills, NJ 07931

MacHovec, Frank.
    Becoming street smart

Library of Congress Catalog Card Number: 93-84524

ISBN: 0-88282-081-8
New Horizon Press

Manufactured in the U.S.A.

1997 1996 1995 1994 1993 / 5 4 3 2 1

ACKNOWLEDGMENTS

My thanks to my wife, who made this book readable, and to Joan Dunphy and New Horizon Press, who moved it from idea to reality.

CONTENTS

Preface

This book was written with two goals in mind: (1) to wake you up, and (2) to scare the hell out of you. Stated more softly, it is to convince you that no one is immune from crime, to help you avoid being a victim, and to help you cope better if you become one. Flight 103, which exploded over Lockerbe, Scotland, the bombing of the World Trade Center in New York City, today's news of crime in your local area—all are hard evidence that crime can occur to anyone, anywhere, at any time.

It is normal to be anxious, fearful, or apprehensive about the possibility of being a crime victim. One way to reduce these feelings is to prepare in advance for such an event. To be forewarned, as the saying goes, is to be forearmed. It *is* possible to reduce the probability of being a crime victim and to reduce the degree of violence if you are attacked.

Being street smart is knowing what could happen to you

or your loved one, wherever you are, whatever you're doing, from the moment you leave home to the moment you return. If you follow the recommendations in this book you will lower your risk of being victimized by crime. This does not mean that you have to stop doing the activities you enjoy. It *does* mean you will have to be more cautious, wary, and suspicious of others. You may for the first time in your life choose to carry a non-lethal personal defense weapon—a whistle, portable alarm, or chemical spray—and train in and practice a system of self-defense. This is the price we pay, the personal cost of crime prevention.

Read and study this book. Review and reread it from time to time. Select other resources from the lists of suggested readings and read more about the subjects that interest you. It will be time invested in improving your safety. Most important, *do something!* Put the recommendations of this book into practice every day. The life you save may be your own, or your loved one's. Nothing will change if you do nothing. If everyone were to use just a portion of what this book recommends, crime would be dramatically reduced.

When you read a newspaper account or see television news coverage of an especially shocking crime, ask yourself these two simple questions: Isn't it enough to make you sick? Is it enough to wake you up and make you do something about it? This book can be your guide on the path to better safety and security for you and your community. As Confucius observed, "When there is peace in the home, there is peace in the community. When there is peace in the community, there is peace in the city, and in the nation, and in the world." It can be so, for you, right now. Read on. Good luck.

Crime and You: Wake Up!

MURPHY'S LAW, MAC'S LAW

If Murphy's Law is "Whatever can go wrong will," Mac's First Law is "If a crime can occur, it will." There are several corollaries to Mac's First Law:

1. Most crimes can be anticipated—and therefore prepared for and prevented.

2. The best crime prevention is not being there—stated another way, avoiding high crime risk places and situations.

3. If you're on a crime scene, knowing what you should and should not do can save your life and property.

4. Now, before it happens, is the time to prepare for the

worst. Whatever happens will not be a total surprise or as upsetting to you.

Mac's Second Law is "Every criminal should be arrested, tried, convicted, and sentenced." It has but one corollary: "Every crime should be reported."

If First Aid is "what to do till the doctor comes," then personal security is "what to do till the police come" or "what to do when there are no police." Many people (you may be one) avoid thinking about crime in personal terms. Like soldiers in combat facing death daily, they choose to believe it won't happen to them. Tragically, in war and crime, it can and does happen to someone, like a random wheel of misfortune. Most crimes strike unexpectedly for victims and witnesses, making it difficult for them to recall and positively identify assailants. The major goal of this book is to help tilt the balance in favor of crime prevention and law and order. But nothing will change if you do nothing about crime. In this and other chapters the what, where, and how of crime will be described, probably in such detail it may be unpleasant for you. You may not want to distrust others or realize how unsafe you are in your everyday life. Many crime victims report, "It happened so suddenly . . . " and "He (or she) seemed like such a nice person." This book will help you evaluate your everyday behaviors to reduce the risk of becoming a crime victim. Equally important, you will learn what you can do to protect yourself and others and reduce crime risk.

FBI statistics estimate a crime is committed in the United States every two seconds, a violent crime every twenty seconds, and a property crime every three seconds. About thirty-five million crimes are committed every year in the United States, according to the latest Department of Justice *National Crime Victimization Survey*. But only one in three crimes are reported. Seventy percent of violent crimes are committed by a hardcore of 6 percent of criminals. Most of them plea-bargain their offenses, and only one in six go to prison. When they do they serve about one-third of their sentences. Most crime victims suffer economic loss—many five hundred dollars or more and from one day to two weeks away from their jobs. Statistically, there has been a slight decrease in crime over the past ten years, from an all-time high of 41.5 million. But this is little consolation if you are a victim.

Whether you are optimistic or pessimistic about crime, it is clear that crime *does* pay for someone, and we pay the bill in property, money, injury, and sometimes our lives. The first step in becoming street smart is to realize *you can be a crime victim at any time, any place, wherever you are, whatever you're doing.* It can be sudden, unexpected, by an assailant known to you, someone you trusted, or a stranger. Ted Bundy, the notorious serial killer, was a gracious, charming person. Some criminals have posed as police or security officers, clergy, or physicians. Other criminals are more direct. Carjackers are likely to approach you in your car on the street in broad daylight. Thieves can rob you day or night in public or secluded places, as you leave or enter your home or car, at a restaurant, in an airport, even on the beach or in a theme park. Women have been raped in their cabin on cruise ships, on trains, and on buses.

You can prepare in advance by rehearsing in real life and in your mind what you would want to do in various crime situations. To do this you will need to take the time to read this book thoroughly and regularly review it to maintain your readiness to react in a crisis. Airline pilots are trained in mock flight simulators to meet every possible emergency so that when an emergency occurs they react quickly and effectively. If you do not take steps to prepare yourself for potential crime situations, the severe stress of a crime can interfere with your ability to escape danger and cause lasting psychological and emotional harm. By reading this book carefully, taking notes, reviewing its suggestions, and applying them in your everyday life, you can develop and put into action your own personal security program.

Most citizens don't take crime seriously. They know it happens and may even know family or friends who have been victimized, but it is still somehow unreal, like a bad dream. Many victims report this "can this really be happening?" shock reaction. When you are in this phase of testing what's real and unreal you are passive, not able or willing to take action, to escape or to fight back. You are at that moment the ideal victim, just what the criminal is seeking. It is important that you wake up and take the threat of crime very seriously—now, before it happens. It is equally important that you realize that just reading about crime does little to prepare you. You should reread these pages and take action to choose among your options in any given crime situation and be ready, willing, and able to take action with all your mental and physical strength. To paraphrase the British philosopher Edmund Burke, "The only thing necessary for the triumph of evil is that good people do nothing."

BE APT!

APT stands for the three steps toward being street smart:

Anticipate
Prepare
Train

Anticipate means to develop an early warning system of potential or real danger. Most people resist this bit of advice but it is in your best interest to *trust no one*. A police officer or priest who congenially chats with you could be a serial killer.

Though very rare, it *has* happened. The person who casually asks directions can be a carjacker or thief. The well-dressed businessman with an attaché case may have just robbed your hotel room. This does not mean to be paranoid, cold, or rude to others. You can and should still be yourself, but with the added awareness that some violent criminals can pass at least initially as warm, friendly people. Many people have a problem with this. Many of us are too trusting. Get over it—we're talking about your survival. Some people may feel you are aloof, but you will be alive and well.

The key to effective anticipation is to be constantly aware of where you are and what could happen. If you do so, you will park your car in clearly visible, well-lighted places. You will walk where more people are, away from concealed places. You will be especially cautious whenever you are alone, wherever you are, whatever you're doing. Do you feel this is unreasonable, that it infringes on your freedom? Would you walk through New York's Central Park alone at 2:00 A.M.? High-crime areas and high-risk situations should be *avoided*. If you must be in such places, do not go there alone. All these are aspects of anticipation.

Prepare is advance planning. It is to answer the question "What would I do if . . . " You should be asking yourself this question frequently as you leave and return home. Later in this book we will discuss personal security devices you may choose to carry, from whistles and chemical sprays to guns. Your legal liability increases with the dangerousness (lethality) of the weapon. The bottom line of preparation is its goal: *escape*. The object is not to be a hero but to remove yourself from danger. Let the police cope with danger.

Being prepared means you have thought about your choices of how to react in advance and are ready to act on the one you feel best meets the situation. When you are prepared you will feel more self-confident. This helps make up for the irritation you might feel because you have to second guess people's motives. Many people find it comforting to have a whistle or spray with them even if they never use them.

Training and Rehearsal complete the APT street safety readiness program. You continue to *anticipate* potential crime situations, are *prepared* by mentally scanning ways to escape or defend yourself, and have drills to *train* yourself so you're ready. As with any other skill, practice makes perfect. But there must be practice. One way to practice is to visually scan while walking or driving, more than you have in the past. This is true on the street, in parking lots, shopping malls, stores, restaurants, even going to, being in, and leaving your workplace. Reflect on possible danger situations as you walk or drive. What could you do? What would you do? The other chapters in this book will provide background information to help you be APT to the dangers and the ways you can cope with them.

If you are a parent or a caregiver responsible for others, being APT to crime is more involved:

*A*ssume nothing, be *A*lert, *A*ware, *A*ttentive.
*P*ractice *P*revention, avoid crime situations.
*T*ake control.

Assume Nothing

Street smart people expect the unexpected and when out in public never fully trust anyone. That is discouraging, especially when you're with those you would otherwise trust. It is sadly true that many, perhaps most, crimes could have been prevented had victims double-checked and taken preventive action. It is better to be safe than sorry; it is worth it even if someone is offended by your distrust. Embarrassment to yourself and others for checking them out is a small price to pay to protect yourself and others against physical and psychological harm or major property loss.

Would you trust these guys?

Mr. A played Little League baseball and was a Boy Scout as a kid, ran on junior and senior high track teams, was elected to the student council and awarded a college scholarship. He worked part-time as a busboy and dishwasher, shoe salesman, security guard, and dorm night manager, and did some volunteer work on a crisis phone line. He earned a bachelor's degree in psychology and went on to law school. People described him as a real "Joe College" guy.

Mr. B, born to a poor family, had a close relationship with his mother. He liked to run errands for teachers at school and earned money doing yard work and emptying garbage cans, mostly for women. He worked summers as a dishwasher in a Cape Cod hotel. He did not smoke or drink and liked to swim. He joined the army, made sergeant in the military police, and his neatness merited him "Colonel's Orderly" twenty-seven times. He was middleweight boxing champ in the U.S. Army, Europe, for two years. At age twenty-two he married a German woman after three years of dating, and they had two children.

Can you imagine yourself chatting with these fellows in an airport waiting area? You may have talked to people much like them. Neither of them looked or acted like crooks. Both were serial killers and extremely dangerous criminals. Mr. A was Theodore Robert "Ted" Bundy, who used his intellect and good looks to charm then kill women. He confessed to twenty-six murders, but may have killed fifty or more. Selecting and killing victims was a habit and skill he enjoyed—a classic psychopath. He preferred coeds with long hair parted in the middle.

Mr. B was Albert Frank DeSalvo, "the Boston Strangler"

or "Green Man," who posed as a repair man in green coveralls to gain entrance to his victims' apartments. In a two-year period he raped and killed thirteen women from twenty to eighty-five years old. His criminal record started at age twelve robbing a newsboy and molesting a child, then grew in time to serial rape-murder.

Both these men had an enormous amount of anger and rage narrowly focused on women. They cleverly disguised it until they had their victims in a place where they could vent their murderous rage. The point is that the most dangerous criminals look and act normal. The only protection against these monsters is to be more cautious in your interaction with others.

Prevent

This step requires that you think in advance about what could happen if a service provider is a criminal. The crime and criminal types described in this chapter and others will provide you with enough information for a realistic preventive attitude. If it makes you a little paranoid, remember the old saying: "You're not paranoid if someone is really out to get you."

Take Control

Taking control means that you take some definite preventive action. This can be done by checking babysitter references, asking for ID from service providers *before* letting them into your home and phoning their central office for confirmation. You do have a dead-bolt lock and chain and/or a peephole on the door, don't you? The time to ponder what you could have done to prevent a crime is before it happens.

THE WORLD OF CRIME

The more you know about crime, criminals, and crime situations the more street smart you will be. What is crime? U.S. Department of Justice definitions will help you understand the varieties of crimes. Knowing them will help you plan how to cope with a crime situation. The two major crime types are personal and household. Personal crimes are those with direct personal contact, attempted or completed, with or without physical contact. They include rape, assault, personal robbery, and personal larceny. Household crimes include burglary (forced or unlawful entry), household larceny (of money or property, such as by intruder, guest, or maid), and motor vehicle theft (unauthorized use or theft).

If you are ever a crime victim, you should know how to describe what happened in terms police use. Here are the most frequent crimes:

Assault

Assault is an unlawful physical attack or threat of an attack, classified as *simple* or *aggravated*. Simple assault is without a weapon, with little or no injury requiring less than two days of hospitalization, and can be attempted, threatened, or completed. Any assault with a weapon is classified as aggravated, even if there is no injury. Serious injury even without a weapon is also considered an aggravated assault. An injury is considered serious if it requires more than two days of inpatient hospital treatment. Rape, completed or attempted, and robbery, completed or attempted, are excluded. Assaults remained fairly constant from 1975 to 1990. In 1975 there were 10 aggravated and 16 simple assaults per 1,000 population. In 1990 there were 8 aggravated and 17 simple assaults per 1,000, a total of 4.7 million victims.

Murder

Murder is intentionally causing death, planned or impul-
sively, with or without provocation, or in the act of committing or attempting to commit another crime. There are
fifty-five murders a day in the United States, more than
twenty thousand a year. Most victims and killers are male and
fifteen to forty years old. *Manslaughter* is causing death with
"extreme provocation" or "without legal justification" (non-
negligent or voluntary manslaughter). To confuse you further,
murder and manslaughter can both apply to a single act if
there is no negligence, preventable accident, conspiring to
commit or solicit murder, or attempted but not completed
murder.

Serial killers, those who kill more than one person and
with regularity, are probably the most frightening of all violent
criminals. It is estimated there are fifty serial killers somewhere
in the United States at a given time, about one per state. Because they travel and by killing more than one person become good at it, they are difficult to apprehend. Most of them
specialize in certain types of victims, and they leave a "signature" or unique style in the way they lure victims, how and
where they kill, and the weapons they use. Jack the Ripper,
never apprehended, preferred street prostitutes. Ted Bundy
liked coeds with long brown hair parted in the middle and
used a "Joe College" nice-guy approach. Albert DeSalvo, the
Boston Strangler, posing as a repair man, preyed on older
women. These killers passed unnoticed on the street, unsus-
pected by most of the people who saw and interacted with
them. Bundy actually served as a volunteer worker on a
phone crisis line.

Serial killers rarely look or seem dangerous, at least on
first impression. They can be like the person next door, or
even like the man or woman of your dreams. Most are

sociable, smooth talkers who do not look at all like the primitive beasts they become when they kill. Upon closer inspection there are signs of imbalance, such as distorted thinking and bizarre sexual fantasies. As children, many themselves were abused, tortured animals or mistreated other children, or set fires.

Victims are most frequently those readily available, the person the killer can most easily entice and manipulate, or one specifically chosen because he or she looks or behaves in a certain way that attracts the killer. Prostitutes are at high risk because they are accessible, easy to pick up and transport to a remote place, and tend not to contact police. Children are more easily deceived and physically overpowered than adults. The unwary, preoccupied, or drunk are vulnerable because of their inattention and lack of critical, defensive thinking.

Rape

Rape is sexualized aggression: forced oral, anal, or vaginal intercourse or forced penetration by penis or object. It can be heterosexual or homosexual. The U.S. Department of Justice defines it as "carnal knowledge through the use of force or the threat of force, including attempts." Statutory rape (without force) is not included in government statistics. Reported rapes occur every six minutes, but most rapes are not reported and therefore not investigated or prosecuted. Reported rape of females age twelve or older has declined from 1.7 per 1,000 in 1975 to 1.0 per 1,000 in 1990. Rape accounts for 154,570 of 4 million violent crimes. Rapists use a weapon in one of five attacks. There will be more on sex crime in Chapter 2.

• • •

Property Crimes

Burglary is unlawful entry—forced, attempted, or by passive intrusion—into a residence, business, property, hotel, or cottage. *Forcible entry* is "breaking in" by damaging property, for example, prying open a door or breaking a window. It is not necessary that anything be stolen (that's theft, a separate unlawful act). *Unlawful entry* is a crime even if the residence or property is unlocked. It is burglary if the intruder has no legal right to be there. There has been a gradual decline in the burglary rate from 92 per 1,000 in 1975 to 54 per 1,000 in 1990. In 1975 there were 32 forcible entries, 41 without force, and 20 attempted forcible entries per 1,000. In 1990 there were 19 forced, 24 without force, and 11 attempted forcible entries per 1,000 in 5.2 million reported incidents.

In 1975 there were 125 reported household larcenies per 1,000 households, and in 1990 the rate had diminished to 87 per 1,000 for a total of 8.3 million households. *Larceny* is theft, attempted or completed, personal or household, without force or illegal entry. Personal larceny is theft or attempted theft of money or property by stealth and further classified as *personal larceny with contact,* such as purse snatching on the street or pickpocketing, or *personal larceny without contact,* such as theft of money or property from a car, hotel room, restaurant, or beach. In 1975 there were 3 larcenies with contact and 93 without contact per 1,000 persons. In 1990 the larceny rate with contact remained the same, and dropped to 65 per 1,000 persons without contact, on a total of 13 million victims.

Robbery is the unlawful taking of money or property, attempted or completed, directly or indirectly, with or without the use of force or a weapon. It is *robbery with injury* if it resulted in less than two days of hospitalized treatment. Robbery declined from 6.8 per 1,000 in 1975 to 5.7 per 1,000 in

1990, when 296,400 robberies were reported.

Motor vehicle theft. There has been no significant change in the rate of motor vehicle theft from 1975 to 1990, averaging 13 completed and 7 or 8 attempts per 1,000 vehicles. There are, however, specific types of motor vehicle crime on the increase, such as carjacking and "chop shop" theft to disassemble vehicles for parts. Thieves can get twice the street value of a stolen car by selling all its parts.

Personal and household crimes. These crimes consistently decreased over the fifteen years from 1975 to 1990. There were 33 violent crimes per 1,000 in 1975, 32 per 1,000 in 1990. Personal crimes were 96 per 1,000 in 1975 and 68 per 1,000 in 1990. Household crimes were 237 per 1,000 in 1975 and 161 per 1,000 in 1990, for a total of 34.4 million cases.

Drug crimes are classified as two types: *trafficking* (manufacture, distributing, selling, smuggling, or storing to sell) and *possession* (at home, in a car, office, or on one's person but not with intent to sell). Alcohol and drug abuse are major contributing factors in a variety of crimes and will be covered in more detail in Chapter 2.

Weapons offense includes the unlawful manufacture, alteration, transport, distribution, sale, trade, or use of a deadly or dangerous weapon or accessory.

Other felonies include receiving stolen goods, multiple recurrent traffic violations, bribery, obstructing justice, escaping from custody, child neglect or nonpayment of child support, and nonviolent sex offenses (pornography, statutory rape, contributing to the delinquency of a minor, pimping, prostitution, or attempts at these).

In a crime situation more than one criminal act can occur. For example, rape can involve use of a weapon, robbery, threat, or assault. This can confuse statistical reporting because there can be several crimes committed in one situation or crime event. U.S. Department of Justice statistics count a crime only once and classify it according to severity. Reporting is like a card game in which the highest-ranked crime is the card that wins and is reported; any other lower ranking crimes go unreported. For example, personal contact and violent crimes rank higher than non-contact, non-violent crimes such as theft. The descending priority of crimes is as follows:

Personal	Property
rape	burglary
robbery	motor vehicle theft
assault	larceny

Some crimes never get listed in the statistics database. Among these are date and spouse rape, spouse/partner abuse, child molesting, and rape that ended in murder and counted only as murder. More than 130,000 women are raped every year, but over 2 million are "battered women" injured in family or domestic violence. Minors who rape or molest often have charges reduced to sexual battery or battery (with the sex offense removed) or the ambiguous "carnal knowledge." In many cases, charges are plea-bargained down to less serious minor offenses carrying lighter sentences. Prosecutors do this to ensure that offenders don't "walk" but get at least some partial charge on their record.

WHERE CRIME OCCURS

Statistics provide helpful information about *where* crimes take place. Most violent crime occurs on a street away from the victim's home and by a stranger (23%). Others occur in the victim's residence (11%), parking lot or garage (11%), the residence of a friend or neighbor (9%), a school or office (5% each), open area (4%), or on public transportation or inside the station (1%). About half of all violent crime occurs five miles or more from the victim's home, one in four inside or very near the victim's residence, and only 3 percent more than fifty miles away. At the time of the crime most victims are engaged in leisure activity outside the home. That is where most armed robberies occur, but one in ten occur in the victim's residence. Robbers who are strangers are likely to carry a gun; non-strangers tend to use a knife. Assault and robbery by those known to victims are more likely to result in physical injury to victims, at about an equal rate for male and female victims. From this information, it is possible to assess your risk of being victimized according to where you are and what you are doing.

Motor vehicle theft—stealing or unauthorized use of a vehicle—is the most reported of all crimes (74% in 1991). It occurs in parking lots or garages (36%), at or near the victim's home (22%), or off the street (20%). This information, and police and victim reports of carjacking, suggest guidelines to prevent vehicle theft and personal injury.

NOW, CHOOSE!

Crime statistics describe the world of crime that surrounds you every day and every night, wherever you are, whatever you're doing. By now you should feel APT to becoming street smart. It will help you decide what you can or would want to do by what others have done when they were crime victims. Department of Justice statistics show that most victims of violent crime (71%) took some action to protect themselves. That percentage is higher for rape victims (82%) and those assaulted (73%) and lower for robbery (58%). Those who resisted did so more often when the attacker was known to them. Men and women take protective action in about equal numbers, but women are less aggressive and instead scream, give an alarm, or get help. Men tend to actively fight an un-armed assailant. The most frequent reason given by those who passively submitted was fear that resistance would enrage the attacker and make him more aggressive.

Victims of violent crimes are more likely to take action to protect themselves than those who report general crime (71% vs. 38% in 1991). Victims twelve to nineteen years old are less likely to report crimes than older victims. When the crime is not successful and there is no injury or loss, victims are less likely to report it. Until *all* crimes are reported the crime rate will remain high. Criminals are not stupid; they know that most crimes go unreported, so there is less deterrent. In this sense *crime does pay*. So, another choice you should make now is to report all crimes. This alerts police to trouble areas and suspects so there can be surveillance and more prompt intervention when someone else is victimized.

An unhappy lesson from the rioting and looting after the Rodney King incident in Los Angeles and the Watts riots years earlier is that police may not be able to restore order or protect public and private property. Even without such a catastrophic event, the time lapse from crime to the arrival of police will vary. Department of Justice statistics analyzed police intervention in 2.7 million violent crimes in 1991. Police were on the scene in 75 percent of cases, did not show up 15 percent of the time, and victims went to the police in 8 percent of cases. So, it is possible police will not show up even when called. Now is the time to decide what you will do in the variety of crimes that can happen to you. You have the advantage of time from now on to carefully reflect on your options, choose alternatives, prepare yourself, and rehearse in your mind and in your behaviors what you will do if and when you become a crime victim.

In a crime situation your highest priority should be to *escape*. If you cannot escape you have only two choices: *resist* or *submit*. You will not have much time to decide. Chances are you will be alone, with no one to help you decide what you could or should do. *Now* is the time to consider your options. "To be forewarned is to be forearmed" as the saying goes, and thinking and planning ahead will provide you with a few seconds more time in a crisis situation to act decisively.

Here are some suggestions:

Resist. This is a judgment call only you can make. You may choose to resist if your life is in danger, you believe there is better than fifty-fifty chance you'll be seriously injured or killed, you are confronted with a deadly weapon and are reasonably certain it will be used against you, or you are attacked and believe it will not stop.

Submit if you feel there's a better than fifty-fifty chance the assailant wants only your money or property, frequently true in robbery and carjacking situations. The reality (which doesn't help) is that some people who resist are not harmed and some who submit are. Crime situations and their danger vary as much as what victims do and do not do. You can only prepare yourself as to what *you* would want to do if it happens to you. The AVOID system will help you with this planning.

THE AVOID SYSTEM

Sit back now, reflect, and take a good, hard look at crime situations that may someday confront you. Prepare *now* and minimize psychological trauma and the chances of physical injury by considering what you would like to be able to do. The AVOID system is a way to do this systematically. Each letter stands for a "prep step" to help prepare you for the worst:

A is for *active avoidance*. The best way to avoid being a crime victim is by not being there. The next best thing is to escape. The longer you remain in a dangerous situation, the greater the chance of being hurt or killed. You can minimize risk by planning and thinking ahead, staying out of high-risk areas, situations, and times; being aware of where and how you walk, stand, sit, and look; and by using a buddy system, having someone with you in risk areas. A also stands for *anticipate*, developing "mental radar," being "up" and "on" to *any* potential risk.

V is for *vigilance,* security awareness, and visual scanning of people, place, and space, the personal security zone around you, using neutral but certain eye contact (aware, not fearful or provocative, avoidant, or submissive). As unpleasant as it may be, when it comes to your life and safety and those you love it is better to trust no one, to consider everyone potentially evil until proven otherwise. Many serious crimes occur when victims trust or "give the benefit of the doubt" to criminals. Serial killers use this natural trust to charm victims to the killing ground.

O is for *orientation* physically and mentally, ensuring an escape route wherever you are and whatever you're doing— an optimal defensive position. If you have a purse, briefcase, umbrella, coat, or security device such as a whistle or chemical spray, carry it in your dominant hand ready for use. *O* also stands for *objectivity*, to see exactly what's there and not what you want to see or are afraid to see. This is the "taking stock" step.

I is for *intent,* assessing a suspect's possible motives and danger potential—a calm, reasoned evaluation of risk potential, the suspect's next move, and your next move: flight (preferred), fight, or submit. This is the "should I, would I, will I" step of considering all possible alternatives, keeping escape first.

D is for *decide* and then to *decisively do* it: resist or submit, fight or flight, go-don't go. Unless you are armed and proficient with a weapon or a black belt in a martial art it's better to surrender weaker objects (coat, purse, briefcase), giving you time to evaluate further and escape, submit (to lessen risk of violence), or attack (if you can win or withdraw safely). The bottom line is: whatever you do, do it well. The best way to do this is to be APT—aware and attentive, prepared in advance, and trained by having rehearsed actions in your mind and being thoroughly familiar with any security devices you choose to carry.

Throughout this book, as various crime situations are described, think of how *you* can apply the AVOID system to protect yourself. Personal security is *personal*—only you can decide what you would want to do and how you can best defend yourself based on your own individual strengths and weaknesses.

PARANOID YET?

By now you should be either irritated that so much is being made of crime and the need to go out of your way to defend yourself, or paranoid that you will be attacked before you close this book. Both are normal reactions and both show good reality contact. It is a shame that people have to be more aware of crime than ever before. As the old saying goes, "You aren't paranoid if somebody's really out to get you," and on the street today there are people who will get you if you are in their way or a prime target. There are crimes every day, everywhere, in homes, offices, and on the street. Sooner or later you or someone you know will be a crime victim. It is a very high statistical probability—a matter of time. If and when it happens you can be a passive victim—which could lead to your death—or you can carefully consider now, while there is time to study and reflect, how much you would want to resist, choose how to do so, and plan and train for it. As we've said, you do not have to be a hero.

The practical goal is to escape unhurt and minimize psychological harm. To do so you may have to take action to protect yourself and your loved ones. That is your right. If you choose this active role you must work at it by mental rehearsal ("what if"), vigilance and visual scanning wherever you are, and further reading and training in self-defense. It is also important to realize there are no rights without responsibility. Reprisal and retribution go beyond escape from harm and self-defense. They occur after the crime. The police and the courts are involved in accountability for crime. That is their business and their legal mandate. Police are far better trained and more knowledgeable than you to take effective action after a crime has been committed. The courts determine the seriousness of offenses and the most appropriate consequences. If you take the law into your own hands or use excessive force to defend yourself, you become part of the problem and not the solution.

USEFUL RESOURCES

Commercial Television

There are weekly television shows helpful in understanding and coping with crime. "Cops" features city, county, and state police in actual crime situations. The types of crimes and police procedures will help you increase your awareness of where and how crimes occur, how victims and witnesses react, and what you would have done in the situation. "America's Most Wanted" dramatizes recent crimes and gives viewers the opportunity to help apprehend suspects still at large through a telephone hotline. More than two hundred suspects have been apprehended with the help of viewers who provided information to the show's hotline. "Prime Suspect" does not dramatize but uses a news approach and an 800 number to receive tips.

Victim Resources

The National Organization for Victim Assistance (NOVA) provides a referral service for victims and training and technical assistance to courts, and sponsors local, state, and national conferences. Write or phone NOVA for more information at 1757 Park Road NW, Washington, DC 20010 (phone: 202-232-6682; FAX: 1-202-432-2255). They operate a twenty-four-hour hotline staffed by crisis counselors at 1-202-462-6682.

Government Publications

There are many free booklets available from the Bureau of Justice Statistics Clearinghouse, Box 6000, Rockville, MD 20850 (phone: 1-800-732-3277). Most of the statistics in this chapter were taken from publications listed below. Order them if you want more information on crime statistics. You can also ask to be put on the mailing list to receive future editions of these useful publications. These are especially recommended:

Chaiken, M. R. (1993). Can drug epidemics be anticipated? *National Institute of Justice Journal, 226,* 23–30.
Compendium of Federal Justice Statistics. Published annually.
Crime in the United States, 1973–1990 trends. NCJ-139564.
Criminal Victimization in the United States, a National Crime Victimization Survey. NCJ-139563.

Drugs and Crime Facts 1992. NCJ-139551.

Federal Criminal Case Processing 1980–1990. BJS Report, September 1992.

Pretrial Release of Felony Defendants 1990. NCJ-139560.

Reaves, B. A. (1992). *Pretrial Release of Felony Defendants, 1990.* Bureau of Justice Statistics Bulletin.

Recidivism of Felons on Probation 1986–1989. NCJ-134177.

Riedel, M., Zahn, M. A., & Mock, L. F. (1985). *The Nature and Patterns of American Homicide.* Research Report. National Institute of Justice.

School Crime. NCJ-131645.

Sourcebook of Criminal Justice Statistics. Published annually. NCJ-137369.

Violent State Prisoners and Their Victims. NCJ-124133.

The FBI also provides publications and information about their Uniform Crime Reports (UCR) widely used for crime reporting. For further information write or phone the FBI, care of Criminal Justice Information Services, 10th and Pennsylvania Avenues NW, Washington, DC 20535 (phone: 202-324-2614).

Oher Useful Publications

Black, H. C. (1979). *Black's Law Dictionary.* St. Paul, MN: West.

Boland, B., Conly, C. H., Mahanna, P., Warner, L., & Sones, R. (1990). *The Prosecution of Felony Arrests, 1987.* Washington, DC: Abt Associates.

Federal Bureau of Investigation (1989). *Crime in the United States.* ICPSR 9394. Washington, DC: FBI.

MacHovec, F. J. (1991). *Private Investigation: Principles and Practice.* Springfield, IL: Charles C. Thomas.

CHAPTER 1: CRIME AND YOU: WAKE UP!

MacHovec, F. J. (1992). *Security Services, Security Science*. Springfield, IL: Charles C. Thomas.

CHAPTER 2

Getting Ready

Chapter 1 should have convinced you that (1) crime is real, (2) crime is everywhere, and (3) crime can happen to you. It might have raised your anxiety level, creating feelings of insecurity that you are more vulnerable to crime than you thought. This chapter should lower your anxiety by describing in detail the materials and methods you can use if you are ever in a crime situation. The intent is to help you plan your own personal security system.

KNOW THYSELF

"Know thyself" was the simple but very profound command inscribed over the entrance to the Oracle of Delphi in ancient Greece. The great philosopher Socrates said that knowing oneself is the beginning of wisdom. It is very important to be aware of any deep-seated bias you have about anyone who might confront you. An exaggerated concern about a person can give you an extra push to take action that is not justified by the situation. One man shot and killed his neighbor because the neighbor's dog urinated on his morning paper. What made the Rodney King beating controversial was not only the question of excessive force but also the fact that he was an African-American and the police were white.

In ancient times it was necessary to undergo a purification ritual to prepare for new learning. You need a "mental shower" to reduce the probability you will overreact to an assailant because of his or her gender, race, religion, national or ethnic origin, or other physical or personal traits. Personal bias is like wearing tinted glasses: you see more than is there. Check yourself *now* for preconceived notions that could tilt the balance toward your use of excessive force. You need to have a clean mental slate as you learn details of how to protect yourself against crime.

KNOW THY ENEMY

Statistical base rates tell us much about crimes and criminals. Recent data show 52 percent of rapists, 84 percent of robbers, and 54 percent of assailants in simple assaults were strangers to their victims. Offenders were known or casual acquaintances in other cases. One in five aggravated assaults were by family members, mostly by the victim's spouse or ex-spouse. For all violent crimes, males were more likely victims than females. A third of violent crime offenders, except in robberies, were perceived by victims to be on alcohol or drugs. Offender age was estimated at between twenty-one and twenty-nine, thirty and older in about a third of cases. When there was more than one offender, age range was estimated as twelve to twenty. Strangers use weapons more than offenders who are known to victims. When non-strangers use a weapon it is more likely to be a knife than a gun.

Decades of research and statistics yield four major reasons for criminal behavior:

1. *Frustration*, a largely emotional reaction that drives a criminal toward spontaneous, impulsive acts.

Examples: One man hits another over the head with a whiskey bottle in a drunken brawl; a husband strangles his nagging wife when she confronts him about his affair with another woman.

2. *Social learning*, a predatory pattern of planned behaviors thought through in advance.

Examples: An ambitious criminal expands his street drug and prostitution business from one neighborhood to the entire city; sexually aroused and armed with duct tape, rope, and a gun, a harmless-looking serial killer knocks on the door of his eleventh rape-murder victim.

3. *Money* to finance an expensive drug habit or an easy way to make a living.

4. *Power.* Many criminals get a high from total control, the power of life and death over victims. Rapists and armed robbers often crave this excitement. Some feel above society and smarter than the police who pursue them.

A typical violent offender profile can be constructed from years of crime statistics. It is most important to realize that few criminals look or seem dangerous. They can look like your friends, neighbors, and co-workers. In some cases, that's who they are. However, crime statistics and years of experience by police and security officers make it possible to construct typical profiles of some offenders.

•   •   •

Sex Crime

Most rapists are driven by one or more of these motives: to vent rage or vengeance; to degrade the victim; to control and dominate; or to fulfill a sick fantasy. Many but not all rapists come from problem families. Troubled mother-son or sister-brother relationships can contribute to a smoldering hate for women who look or act like the hated person. A sixteen-year study of one thousand rapists yielded three major types, each with a distinctive style (Olson, 1989):

1. *"Gentlemen rapists"* are motivated by a compulsion to dominate and control. They usually abduct by surprise and transport victims to a secluded place. They often have a prior record of theft, robbery, burglary, and nuisance offenses. Multiple rapes are typical of this type of offender.

2. *Anger rapists* hate and resent victims and attack suddenly and forcefully with verbal and physical abuse. They may kill if they lose control. Anger rapists tend to be repeat offenders and often have reckless driving and disturbing the peace charges.

3. *Sadistic rapists,* the least common but most dangerous, are "lust murderers," excited by total control of victims and bizarre, usually ritualistic behaviors such as in the Jeffrey Dahmer case and in the movie *Silence of the Lambs.* Bondage, torture, mutilation of specific body parts, and strangulation are common. Sadistic rapists tend to be avid readers of crime stories, and most have kinky fantasies that started in childhood.

Many rapists are married, and most have access to willing sex partners without criminal force. Most were voyeurs ("peeping Toms") or exhibitionists ("flashers") and like pornography and crime stories. They tend to be insecure, inadequate loners, immature and impulsive, with little insight into themselves and others, and see the world as threatening.

They choose victims who are available, vulnerable, and have certain physical features such as age, height, hair color or style, or eye color. Rapists do not necessarily choose victims based on sexual attraction.

Child molesters, or *pedophiles,* are usually but not always older than their victims. Offenders can be male and female, single or repeat offenders, heterosexual or homosexual, violent or non-violent. Molesters, compared to rapists, tend to be more passive offenders, using persuasion, manipulation, or fear rather than aggression, though some physically overpower smaller, younger prey. There are several types:

- *Fixated* molesters seek victims of a certain age.
- *Regressed* molesters have age-appropriate sex but also have sex with minors, usually under stress.
- *Morally indiscriminate* molesters are "users and abusers" of others.
- *Sexually indiscriminate* molesters are "try-sexuals"— they'll try anything to vent and relieve their sex drive, either out of boredom, fantasy, fascination, or experimentation.
- *Inadequate molesters* are social misfits, eccentric, or mentally ill (psychotic, senile, or retarded).
- *Situational molesters* do not usually or consistently prefer minors but may choose a minor as a victim if the opportunity presents itself.
- *Preferential molesters* are specifically attracted to minors and are multiple offenders.

Alcohol and Drug Abusers

Half of those charged with simple and aggravated assault had been drinking. A third of reported rape victims thought their assailants were under the influence of alcohol or drugs. In recent years there have been over a million arrests for drug violations in the United States, a fifty percent increase since 1982. Postal inspectors make 1,500 or more arrests a year for illegal drugs sent by mail. The DEA confiscates 150,000 pounds of cocaine, 2,500 pounds of heroin, over 200,000 pounds of marijuana, and 29 million doses of stimulants every year. U.S. Customs confiscates 170,000 pounds of cocaine annually.

Illegal drugs are a big business worldwide. Drug abuse and trafficking are among the most under-reported crimes, not considered bad enough by otherwise law-abiding citizens to be reported. Police estimate that if all dealers were arrested today there would be enthusiastic replacements on the street the next day. Youths are used as carriers and runners to lessen dealer exposure and because minors get reduced sentences. "Crack" cocaine is now more cheaply made and more plentiful. Crack cocaine users often spend more than a thousand dollars a week, driving them to crime to finance the habit.

More bad news: there is a greater variety of drugs to abuse. The side effects of some of them weaken self-control, distort reality, and lead to aggressive behaviors and trancelike violence. Sensitivity to pain can be lowered so that direct body shots by police gunfire won't stop abusers. Often there is little or no memory of the violence. Heavy drug users can become paranoid and delusional, aggressive or suicidal, and unpredictable. Many drug abusers also have mental disorders.

You should know the effects of street drugs on the mind and body to tell if an assailant seems to be under the influence. If so, charges of illegal possession or use of drugs can be added to charges for any crime committed. Most users say they abuse drugs to escape from reality or for a high they can't get any other way. Here's a quick overview of mental and physical symptoms of drug abuse:

Alcohol at its worst lowers the threshold for emotional outbursts and violence to others or to oneself (impulsive suicide). Drunks look bleary-eyed, have slowed reflexes and thinking, slurred speech, clumsy movements, and rapid heart rate.

Opioids. Heroin has been the most common opium source for many years. It gives an ecstatic good mood or high but, over time, indifference and depression. A powerful pain reliever, heroin users can be hit, even shot, without stopping them. Most obvious symptoms of opioid use are flu-like symptoms of sniffling and red teary eyes, and also restlessness, yawning, itchy skin, nausea, and vomiting. Heroin can be injected, sniffed, or smoked. Some other names include "bang," "bingo," "blackjack." IV users are called "channel swimmers," "cookers," or "mainliners" who "shoot up" or "crank up."

Cocaine can be sniffed, smoked, swallowed, or injected. Users "do a line" or "hitch up the reindeer." Street names include "coke," "crack," "base," "snow," "nose candy," "blow," "powder," "toot," "pop," "sniff," "snort," and "White Christmas." Coke has become the street drug of choice and there are "rock" or "base" houses to meet increased demand. Smoking coke is called free-basing, ghost busting, or chasing. "Crack" cocaine, or "rock," is a relatively new form of cocaine. It is cheap and easy to produce and powerful in its effect.

Marijuana can be smoked or swallowed and is weaker in strength and effect than heroin. Other names include "grass," "weed," "roach," "stick," "joint," "tea," and "toke." Users "mow the grass" or have "a tea party" with "Puff the dragon."

Sedatives. These are "downers," and like alcohol they depress the nervous system with similar signs of abuse. Abusers look and act "dumb," slowed down, and confused.

Stimulants. These are "uppers," mostly amphetamines, that give people instant energy and euphoria—and users show it. Users will be restless, constantly on the move with quick, often jerky movements, excessive sweating, trembling, and dilated pupils. A frequent psychological feature is paranoia (excessive suspicion of others). Smokable crystal methamphetamine, known as "super speed," "ice," or "U4Euh," costs more than cocaine but is easily "home cooked," more difficult to detect, and according to many in the drug subculture, produces better highs. It is the child of "speed" or "crank" used in the 1960s by bikers, flower children, athletes, and students cramming for exams. "Cat" is the latest amphetamine, stronger, cheaper, and even easier to make. Among the most dangerous stimulants is PCP, or phencyclidine. Also called "angel dust," "krystal," "peep," or "hog," it can be taken orally, snorted, smoked, or injected. Persons on it can overreact to psychotic proportions and be extremely violent or sit robot-like with a blank stare, thinking off and on like a dimming and brightening light bulb.

Hallucinogens. LSD (d-lysergic acid diethylamide) is the classic and is coming back into street use. Others include mescaline, psilocybin (magic mushrooms), and methamphetamine (STM, DOM, DMT). On these, a person breaks from reality into a dream world of fantasy where real and unreal are mixed together. They can for a time lose their minds (toxic psychosis) or be extremely violent and not remember it later. Their speech rambles, they may hallucinate (hearing voices as well as seeing things) or be dizzy or nauseous.

Volatiles are substances sniffed, such as glue, gasoline, "poppers" (amyl nitrate), "beaut" (butyl nitrate), "laughing gas" (nitrous oxide), or carbon dioxide (CO_2). Most of these inhaled chemicals act as anesthetics, and abusers report feeling no pain. Symptoms are due to oxygen loss, and death by heart failure can occur. Volatiles are among the most brain-damaging drugs.

Some abusers mix these drugs. It's called "dusting." This is very dangerous because the effect can be additive and kill. A "speedball," "goofball," or "dynamite" is a blend of heroin and cocaine. A "Frisco special" or "Frisco speedball" is a mix of cocaine, heroin, and LSD. Cocaine and PCP is a "space cadet" or "tragic magic." PCP and marijuana is "zoom" or "wac." Heroin and marijuana is an "atom bomb." Marijuana and insecticide is "fuel," and marijuana and alcohol is "Herb and Al."

Typical drug abusers you are most likely to see are the marginally employed, street people, scofflaws, and people who feel above the law. The misery from this illegal activity has a ripple effect, a crime wave that covers the community. Desperate addicts can be extremely dangerous to anyone who resists giving them the money or property they need for their next fix. Senseless violence from temporarily deranged drug abusers can victimize anyone, anywhere, from innocent children to the elderly. Addicts are treated in hospital emergency rooms and detox centers many times on a regular repeat basis at considerable expense in time and money. Crack babies born with drug addiction require additional medical care and are likely to need mental health services in later years. Drug abusers lose jobs and marriages and neglect or abuse their children.

USE OF FORCE

To decide what to do in a crime situation requires that you *assess risk*. If someone steals your lawn mower when you're away, all you can do is report it and ask neighbors if they saw anything. If someone picks your pocket or snatches your purse and runs away, it may be better to observe him or her and report it to police. If you run after the crook, what do you do when you catch up? Do you have a weapon? Are you sure the thief does not? If it's a serious or violent crime and you are reasonably certain you can't escape, do you submit or fight back? Some victims have been killed passively submitting and some have been killed actively resisting.

Knowing exactly what to do in a crime situation can be a very difficult judgment call. You must make a split-second cost-benefit analysis at a time of severe stress. By reading and rereading this book you should be better able to make a more informed judgment, based on common sense and reason, than if you did not think about it at all beforehand. Your decision as to what to do and not do depends on the seriousness of your predicament, the likelihood the criminal will injure or kill you if you do not submit. To confuse you further (sorry, but you *must* consider it), if the assailant shows clear intent to kill you, why not fight for your life rather than die passively? That is the most extreme situation you could ever be in. Most crimes will not present these last-resort alternatives; they take less than a minute, and most victims survive unhurt. If that was always the case this book would not be needed. Avoiding and preventing crimes that injure or kill victims are the goals of this book.

Deciding whether or not you want to arm and defend yourself is a judgment call only you can make. It is best to consider now what you would do in a high-risk confrontation. If your life is in danger and there is an escape route, will you submit, try to escape even if reasonably certain you won't succeed, or stand and fight for your life? You should choose actions equal to the threat—just the right amount of force to control the situation, prevent escalation, and allow you to escape. If you use excessive force you may later find yourself in court, expected to prove your response was reasonable, appropriate, and based on a fear and belief that your life was in danger. What weapons are most used by criminals? There are more than twenty thousand murders every year, and the weapons used in order of frequency are guns (66%), knives (16%), hands or feet (6%), blunt striking objects (5%), strangulation (2%), fire (1%), asphyxiation (0.5%), and poison (0.1%).

Police are trained in a *use of force continuum*. This makes it easier for them to estimate the minimal force to control a crime situation. It is a graduated application of three levels of force (none, ordinary, and extraordinary) that match the criminal's degree of aggression. It will help you develop your own personal security plan to know and reflect on this continuum:

Force Level	Defensive Options
No Force (cooperative level)	1. Controlled Confrontation (verbal)
	2. Body Language (nonverbal)
	3. Verbal Persuasion
	4. Contact Control
Ordinary Force (resistant level)	5. Joint restraints
	6. Weapon-assisted leverage
	7. Nerve center controls
	8. Weapon-assisted pain
	9. Chemical irritant (spray)
	10. Electrical Device (stun gun)
	11. Intimate impact weapon (kubotan)
Extraordinary Force (assaultive level)	12. Extended impact weapon (nightstick)
	13. Weaponless debilitating technique
	14. Service firearm
	15. Supplemental firearm

Cooperative level. Most police confrontations occur at this level when there is verbal and nonverbal communication between you and your assailant. You can exert control by positioning yourself where you are clearly visible, making certain eye contact, and verbally and nonverbally showing that you are aware of the potential and ready to act (defensive options 2 and 3).

Resistant level. This phase is in two levels: reluctance of the assailant to withdraw, or clear resistance of the assailant such as with loud voice or dramatic, threatening gestures. There is still no physical contact between you.

Assaultive level. This behavior involves definite physical contact and occurs at two levels: when the assailant strikes out or throws objects, or extreme life-threatening attack such as shooting at you or lunging with a knife.

DEFENDING YOURSELF

Deadly or *lethal force* is that which is intended to cause serious injury or death. Force is *reasonable* if it is appropriate, just enough to subdue and deter an assailant and prevent injury to you. You may see it as ironic that you are legally liable for any injury you cause an assailant unless you can prove you feared for your life. The legal test is the "reasonable person" rule, which stipulates that anyone else in the same situation would use the same degree of force. It is unreasonable if other reasonable persons would consider it inappropriate or excessive. A *deadly* or *lethal weapon* is a "firearm or other weapon, device, instrument, material, or substance, whether animate or inanimate, which in the manner used is known to be capable of producing death or serious bodily injury," according to *Black's Law Dictionary*. Some courts have ruled AIDS to be a deadly weapon when a person knowingly infected with it intentionally spreads it to others.

You are legally responsible for any weapon or object used as a weapon (for example, gun, spray, bat, or bottle). It is a definite plus if you have taken and can document training in the use of whatever weapon you carry. Liability is proportionate to the length of training, its content, recency, supervised practice, and for guns, range firing. In most states guns or deadly force are justified only if your life or the life of someone else is in clear and imminent danger and there is no other alternative. Gun use or other deadly force should *always* be the very last resort. If there is any reasonable possibility you could have escaped and not used lethal force, it will be difficult in court to justify doing so.

Guns and knives are legally classified as deadly or lethal weapons because they can kill, and using them suggests intent to kill or seriously injure. If an assailant uses a lethal weapon the charges will be more serious and sentencing more severe. If *you* use a weapon to defend yourself, you should be able to justify its use. You may feel that Charles Bronson's vigilante actions against criminals in the *Death Wish* movie series was morally justified, but it was very definitely illegal. You are not allowed to carry a gun unless you are a sworn law enforcement officer or have a concealed weapons permit from your local court.

You are most likely to have a gun in your face in armed robbery situations for your money or property, but shootouts can occur anywhere. In California, police had to shoot an armed gunman in the main library of a major city. Fleeing to the roof, the gunman was shot and fell five stories to the street. Two bodies were found later, shot and killed by the gunman before police arrived. There are many senseless shootings. Motorists have been shot in carjackings even when not resisting. There are drive-by shootings day and night. Some are drug deals that go wrong, but others are thrill killings. A sixty-year-old man in Maryland was shot and killed just walking along a quiet street near his home. Being street smart is to be aware and vigilant wherever you are, whatever you're doing.

Statistics on criminals who shoot police give us some idea of the typical profile of really dangerous persons. If they shoot at armed, uniformed police they will likely not hesitate to shoot you. FBI research reports that about half of the criminals who shot police had killed or attempted to kill someone else before. One in five had assaulted a police officer or resisted arrest beforehand. Only 3 percent had no prior criminal history. Three of four routinely carried a weapon: 34 percent in their belt while driving; 20 percent under the car seat; and 12 percent on the seat next to them. Three of four had been drinking or using street drugs at the time of the shooting.

The typical police killer is a white male in his midtwenties, a high school graduate, about half from violent or dysfunctional families and of **average** financial means. Six of ten police shootings occur at night, only one in ten in the morning. Four of ten officers killed were making an arrest or in a crime situation, two in ten were responding to disturbance calls, one in ten were transporting a prisoner, and another one in ten were investigating suspicious persons or situations. This gives you some idea of the when, where, how, and who of street violence.

LETHAL WEAPONS

Guns

Guns are considered by police and courts to be the most lethal and most dangerous use of force. They are *not recommended* unless you are thoroughly familiar with legal implications, have mastered and are proficient with your weapon, and regularly practice with it at a firing range. Before you decide to buy a gun, consider the negatives. Unlike in the movies, assailants do not always fall immediately to the ground when shot. This is especially true of drug abusers. If you miss, the bullet can ricochet off the street, a wall, or the floor and hit or kill an innocent bystander. If you kill an assailant a court will consider whether you used reasonable or excessive force. A gun can also be taken from you and used against you. Under severe stress you may accidentally shoot yourself as you draw the gun from purse, pocket, or belt, or when awakened from sleep in the middle of the night. And try as you will to keep guns out of the reach of children, kids have an uncanny ability to find them. Once a gun is fired there is no way to stop or slow the bullet. Finally, guns are popular items for thieves to steal, easily concealed and sold on the street regardless of the most stringent control laws.

If you still want a gun despite these negatives, decide on a revolver or semi-automatic of a caliber (bullet diameter), size, and weight that best fits your hand so you can use it well. Decide between single- or double-action. Single-action (SA) means you have to pull the hammer back to fire the first shot on an automatic and every shot on a revolver. Double-action (DA) guns are fired only by pulling back the trigger, though many can be fired single-action as well. Trigger pull varies from about three to over ten pounds of pressure. In most states and nations you can't carry a gun without a concealed weapons permit from the court jurisdiction in which you live. Usually this entails fingerprinting, police investigation, an appropriate reason in writing, and a judge's review and approval. In most areas you don't need a permit if the gun remains in your residence for personal protection except for a permit for initial purchase.

What's the best gun for you? A 2-inch barrel "snub-nose" or "snubby" .38 Special revolver is a good, reliable weapon, easy to operate, maintain, and check if loaded. Its main disadvantage is that it holds only five or six bullets. Automatic pistols are more popular, and today's favorites are 9-mm and .40-caliber Smith & Wessons. Their greatest disadvantages are that they jam more than revolvers, you can't tell how many bullets are in the gun, and you have to pull back the slide or receiver (top part) to load the first bullet. Bullet capacity should not be a priority. Police are involved in more shootouts than private citizens and in most cases fire only one and seldom more than three shots.

If you have little or no experience with guns and want to buy and use one, visit a gun dealer several times to familiarize yourself with them. Shop price as you would any other purchase.

Some suggestions: .380 ACP automatics are smaller and less expensive. They include the Beretta 86, Bersa, Colt Government model, Davis, and Sigarms P230. Or try the .38 Special in 2" or 4" barrels (Colt detective special, Smith and Wesson chief's special or J or K frame, Rossi, Ruger, Taurus) or 9-mm or .40 S&W (Auto Ordnance, Glock, Ruger, Smith and Wesson, Taurus). Look at full-sized and compact models. Make and caliber of a handgun is a personal choice. Generally, name brands are more reliable and more easily serviced locally. Stainless steel or Parkerized (dull black) finishes are rust resistant and many people feel they look better. Custom grips fit the gun to your hand better and can improve handling and accuracy. They are worth the money. Trijicon "night sights" cost an extra one or two hundred dollars and glow in the dark, an advantage when lighting is poor. Inexpensive do-it-yourself glow paint to touch up front and rear sights is available.

While a bullet as small as a .22 can kill, police have emptied their guns on criminals insensitive to pain from street drugs. Such people have kept coming untill they dropped from loss of blood. So, it's better to use something between

.380 ACP and .40-caliber S&W. Heavier calibres such as the .357, .44 magnum, .45, and 10-mm are not well suited to personal protection. To accommodate the larger bullets these guns are big, heavy, more difficult to aim and hold on target, and kick like a mule. Use only ammunition from major manufacturers (CCI, Federal, Remington, and Winchester). Avoid reloads. They void most manufacturer's warranties and have a higher jam and misfire rate. Metal-jacketed hollow-point bullets have the most stopping power because they mushroom open on impact.

After you buy your gun, you should be trained in its use and practice at a firing range at least quarterly, preferably monthly. Use a large silhouette (torso) target and fire a formal course such as fifty rounds (one box) at seven, fifteen, and twenty-five yards. Pause between single shots, then between pairs, then between every six shots, firing one round every second. Regular practice reduces the probability of clumsy handling, missing your target, or shooting yourself or someone else accidentally. Practice clearing jams. Keep your gun clean and serviced. Popular cleaning kits are produced by Hoppe's, Kleen-bore, Otis, Outers, and Section 8. Many people enjoy target shooting and you can participate in non-professional matches sponsored by gun manufacturers, local clubs, and the National Rifle Association. It's a good way to maintain and improve your proficiency.

Gun safety can never be overdone. Every gun is considered loaded until you personally and carefully check to be sure that it isn't. Never point a gun at anyone you do not consider a potential target. Every child accidentally shot playing with a gun is a preventable accident. Some gun experts recommend locking a gun in one place and bullets elsewhere, especially if there are children or others in the area. Alternatives include locking the gun in a bedside table or office desk except when you are there, using a small locking device that fits inside the trigger guard, and an alarm box that sounds a 98-decibel squeal if the gun is moved. Risk of accidental firing is increased while loading and unloading; you should be especially careful whenever doing so.

If You Must Shoot

Shooting anyone is a crisis situation no one should be faced with. As we've stressed, it's always a last resort. In the worst-case scenario you are faced with an assailant with a deadly weapon, unable to escape, and believe if you do not take action you will be killed. Even then, you can and should be talking before you shoot, something like "Stop or I'll shoot" or "I have a gun, put your hands up." It may seem melodramatic, but it has stopped assailants and makes clear your good-faith attempt to avoid firing. If the assailant is not armed and you shoot, you can be charged with excessive force, shooting an unarmed person.

Shoot only to save your life, to stop an armed attack. Aim for the middle of the torso. The object is *not* to shoot to kill but to *stop* the assailant. Before any of this happens you or others should have phoned the police so you know they are on the way. Wait for them if you can before taking the law into your own hands.

If you have a gun you need to be combat ready, similar to police and military readiness:

1. *Know your gun.* In a life-or-death confrontation your gun is your best friend. Get a feel for when it is empty and loaded, safety on or off, so that it becomes second nature to you and you can safely and deliberately handle and operate it at any time, at home, work, or play. Know how to clear jams. Always keep your trigger finger off the trigger and along the trigger guard until you decide to fire.

2. *Know where you are.* Visually scan the scene. Seek

cover if possible to protect you from the assailant shooting back. Sneak peeks from different heights or places. You could be shot the second time you look from the same place. Know your field of fire: "soft" (windows, inside doors, drywall), which bullets can go through; and "hard" (outside walls, street), which bullets can bounce off; and distant, where bullets go if you miss. Don't stand in front of light sources; they provide your assailant with a convenient silhouette target.

3. *Know the enemy.* Burglars usually work in teams, so the person you see may not be alone. Rapists usually work alone and are usually armed. See any weapons? Any sign of alcohol or drug abuse? You may be able to talk down a drunk but not someone on PCP with a weapon.

4. *Observe closely.* Pay special attention to the assailant's hands—where they are, what they're doing, and what's in them.

5. *Take precautions.* Any assailant who submits to you should be ordered to raise his hands and clasp them behind his head, then kneel down and lie face down on the floor until police arrive and take over. Do not stand within reach. Avoid conversation.

6. *Mentally rehearse and prepare.* Sudden stress can distort perception and judgment. Think ahead of the extreme situations in which you would shoot someone. Going over "what if" mental dramas helps prepare you for the real thing. At the range, try jogging in place until you're breathing fast and starting to sweat, then shoot. This gives you some idea how you might react in a crisis situation.

Still want a gun? If you do, re-read and reflect on the information here so that you will behave safely and responsibly, acting as part of the solution rather than adding to the crime problem.

●   ●   ●

Knives

Knives differ in style (pocket, hunting, kitchen), operation (folded or fixed blade), and blade length. Knives over a certain minimum length are illegal to carry in most states except for campers and hunters in legal hunting and outdoors areas. The average hunting knife, legal for hunters in the field, is illegal on the street. Collapsible switchblade knives can jam shut, snap back on your own hand, or be taken from you and used against you. To use a knife you must move in close to the assailant, a position of highest risk to you as victim and defender and therefore *not recommended*. An assailant who uses a knife may be good at it—better than you. You aren't Zorro! Few knives are used these days on the street. Guns are the weapon of choice by criminals and are more frequently used.

NON-LETHAL WEAPONS

Non-lethal weapons are preferable to guns and knives because they deter crime and do not permanently injure or kill. There are three types suitable for personal security protection: chemical sprays, electroshock devices, and the kubotan. *Check local laws to ensure it is legal to own and carry them.* FAA regulations prohibit them in airports beyond security gates and on aircraft. They are illegal in some states; in others, permits are required.

Chemical Sprays

Chemical sprays are aerosol (air dispersal) sprays of powerful chemicals that disable assailants without permanent injury to them. There are three types: CS, or tear gas; CN, or "Mace"; and OC (oleoresin capsicum), or pepper spray. Sprays are used at arm's length without your coming into physical contact with the assailant. They are *distancing weapons,* keeping an assailant away from you, temporarily disabled, without permanent injury. This gives you time to escape and alert police. You should spray and run. Before you buy a chemical spray, check local laws—such sprays are not legal in all states and are prohibited in airports.

To use a chemical spray, hold the can upright in your dominant or strong hand, aim at the assailant's lower face, and spray in a one-second burst in tight, left-to-right or circular motion as you would paint furniture. This ensures enveloping the assailant's mouth, nose, and eyes, the mucous membranes most sensitive to the chemical solution. In a brisk wind or in tight spaces, sprays can blow back on you. To overcome this, manufacturers offer these chemicals in three dispersant types: pinstream, spray, and mist. Mist is most effective but also the most subject to blow back in wind or closed spaces. Pinstream is the most accurate delivery but least effective because it takes a second or two for the chemical to vaporize. Spray is a good balance of effective aim, minimal action time, and maximum effect.

Tear gas (CS) and Mace (CN) are not recommended because they take a few seconds to be effective, do not always work on drug abusers or the mentally disturbed, and can remain active in the air in your car or home for hours or days. Pepper spray *is* recommended because it is the quickest acting of all chemical sprays. The pepper spray "burns like hell" and involuntarily slams eyes shut and blinds the assailant for a few minutes, enabling you to escape. A one percent spray is as effective as five percent or stronger, the only difference being recovery time afterward. Sprayed assailants will have difficulty catching their breath for fifteen to forty-five minutes and a burning sensation in the eyes for an hour. Pepper spray will not only deter humans but also be effective against aggressive dogs, bears, and bees.

A one-by-four-inch pepper spray canister is easily carried, especially with a built-in belt clip, and costs less than twenty dollars. Some pepper sprays also contain Mace (CN), combining the best features of both, but remember that Mace can contaminate a car or room for hours. Some sprays are available with visible orange-red dye or ultraviolet dye visible only under black light, to identify criminals apprehended later. Buy only units with hinged safety lids to prevent accidental discharge, such as Peppergard. Without a safety lid it is possible to discharge the spray in your purse or pocket as you rummage for keys or change. Another advantage of the safety lid is that you can spray only when the canister is pointed away from you.

Do not carry the spray unit on your car keyring, because it will not be available to you while driving or while parked with the keys in the ignition. If it is on your keyring it might also go off as you start the car. Carry the unit firmly in your dominant hand to and from your car and home for quick use if confronted by an assailant. To ensure effective use when needed, fire a short one-second blast in an open outdoor area every other month. Gently shake the unit once a week to keep the unit charged. Replace chemical spray units annually. Do not leave aerosol spray cans in direct sunlight or in closed cars during summertime—they will explode above 130 degrees. Don't ever playfully spray anyone except an assailant—the effects of the spray aren't funny. The antidote to recover from pepper spray is fresh air, and flooding the face with cold water dilutes the pepper and relieves burning. A garden hose is ideal. Cold compresses and Q-tips to the corners of eyes help.

Stun Guns

Electroshock devices or stun guns are handheld high-voltage battery-powered electrical shocking weapons. Underwriters Laboratories (UL) classifies them as non-lethal, but they are not legal in all communities—check before buying one. About the size of an electric shaver (six-by-two-by-one-inch), they are available with a variety of discharge shocks from 40,000 to 120,000 volts. They require physical contact of the gun's two metal prongs against the assailant's body. Their maximum effect is to disable assailants with uncontrollable muscle contractions, neuromuscular weakness, loss of balance, and disorientation from five to fifteen minutes. Poor contact through heavy clothing or a weak battery may produce only a sting, agitating a drug-crazed or mentally disturbed assailant. If the battery is very low or dead there will be no shock at all.

Unless you use a wrist strap, the stun gun can be taken from you and used against you. They are not easily concealed. If despite these negatives you want a stun gun and they are legal in your community, buy one with a wrist strap and a fail-safe trigger to prevent accidental discharge, and check and replace the battery regularly. Avoid holsters—it takes time to remove and use the stun gun. Carry it at your side to and from your car or home and place it on the passenger seat for quick access if driving alone. A purse or coat pocket will serve as a good, handy holster. Stun guns cost fifty dollars and up. I personally do not recommend them.

Kubotan or "Billy Stick"

The kubotan is a solid cylinder about one inch in diameter and six inches long, usually made of the same hard plastic as police nightsticks (polycarbonate), with several grooves for firm grip and two metal rings at one end to which car and house keys are attached. Within arm's length of an assailant it can be used as a flail, striking at an assailant's face. Enough skin cells can be picked up on keys for a DNA match and any scratches on the face can help confirm identification later. Up close, the kubotan can also be used as an impact weapon to eyes or the sensitive area between the neck and collarbone. Kubotans cost about five dollars. I recommend one if you choose to become aggressive *and* become proficient in its use.

You should practice with your kubotan so that you will be able to use it well. Grasp it at the center of the handle. Swing the keys in small circles to get used to its feel and balance. It's something like casting a fishline, but the "hook" is at the end of the rod. Empty beer cans are good targets for practice. Strike in a flailing action in a small arc with maximum strength, like throwing a small ball. The more keys on the outer ring, the greater the impact. Learn to carry the kubotan at the ready in a pocket or purse with the handle inside out of sight and the keys hanging outside. When you approach your car have a firm "fist grasp" on the handle and your car key lightly held between thumb and index finger. Unlock and enter the vehicle with key in this same position and the kubotan firmly gripped for instant use. If attacked and your assessment of the situation is to fight back, let go of the key and with the kubotan firmly in your dominant hand flail at the assailant's face. This gives the attacker the opportunity to back off. If the assailant does not, use the non-key end of the kubotan that is protruding a few inches outside your clenched fist to punch him or her in the eye. Such drastic action and use of force should only be taken if you feel your life is in danger. The Common Law rule is to use just enough force to deter the criminal.

Whistle and Screecher Alarms

Lung-powered handheld whistles, aerosol or battery-powered "screechers," and passive infrared detectors are portable audio alarms. They are easily carried and can be used effectively by children as well as adults. Safe and easy to use, they are recommended for joggers, walkers, and shoppers in highly visible public places. They get attention when there are people around, but they are useless in remote locations where there is no one to hear and respond to them.

Whistles can be safe, effective deterrents, used by children as well as adults. The loudest hand whistle is the Storm All-Weather Safety Whistle, used by police, military, lifeguards, skin divers, and referees. Its shrill tone and 95 decibels can be heard over high wind and crowd noise, even one hundred feet underwater. It clears itself of sand, dirt, or mud and is available in yellow, orange, or black, with matching lanyards. This is an ideal defensive device for children. Cost is eight dollars or less. Write to All-Weather Safety Whistle Co., P.O. Box 8615, St. Louis, MO 63126.

Screechers are aerosol or battery-powered audio alarms that emit a loud, shrill tone. Aerosol types are as small as one-by-three-inch cylinders, will do twenty to thirty short blasts, and cost less than ten dollars. Battery-powered types can be attached to handbags so as to go off if pulled from you with continuous shrill tone. They cost from twenty dollars to over one hundred dollars. The electronic type can come with a combination firing sequence of pull-pin and squeeze-push so an assailant can't turn it off. Test fire your unit once a month. Replace aerosols annually. Screechers are recommended.

Passive infrared detector alarms are battery-powered portable detectors the size of a pocket radio or Walkman that emit an electronic screech when triggered by the warmth of a body (animal or human). They can be placed in your car or hotel room to emit a constant loud alarm or a gentler beep. The beeper is helpful at work if you are alone, to announce the approach of anyone. If it is an assailant, he or she won't know whether it's a central alarm to the police or your own pocket security device. Detectors cost fifty dollars or more.

Blackjacks, Brass Knuckles, and Exotica

Blackjacks are short leather clubs filled with lead pellets and are illegal in most communities. They are aggressive contact weapons and do not offer the safety or distance of chemical sprays. Nunchakus, spring-loaded metal batons, brass knuckles, and other exotic martial arts devices are also illegal and require training and skill in their use. They look flashy in the movies, but when you are under stress you can injure yourself with these weapons. Using contact weapons increases your legal liability for injury you inflict on others. In court, your use of exotic weapons, especially illegal ones, even in self-defense, can be used by an assailant's attorney to paint you as the aggressor rather than as the victim.

Martial Arts

Martial arts require considerable investment of time, regular practice, and exercise to develop and maintain skill. In danger situations, your response can be automatic, controlled, and precise using a martial art. Learning a martial art can bolster your self-confidence as well as help keep you physically fit and emotionally less subject to stress from fear and apprehension. It certainly wouldn't interfere with the other preventive practices described in this chapter.

So What's Best?

Though chemical sprays, stun guns, and kubotans are considered non-lethal, there is always the chance someone can suffer an injury coincident with their use. If you are in the ironic position of being sued by an assailant who claims injury, the burden of proof will be on you to show that you acted in a reasonable manner and used appropriate force equal to the threat to your life and property. If you can document training in the use of the defensive device used, you will greatly strengthen your case.

Chemical sprays keep assailants at a safer distance and do not involve contact or aggressive action by you. For this reason, they are preferred to contact weapons. You may want to have both a kubotan keyring and a chemical spray—carried separately. If both are on your keyring and you are carjacked with keys in the ignition, both weapons are beyond reach. Carrying pepper spray in a coat pocket or on your belt puts the spray within easy reach while you are driving. If you prefer something less offensive than pepper spray, consider an aerosol or electronic screecher alarm.

THE ZEN OF SELF-DEFENSE

Zen is an ancient philosophy that started in China and later spread to Japan. It has been applied to sports as a form of meditative awareness. For example, tennis players can become so proficient that while playing, "all is one"—they are part of their rackets and the ball. In ancient times archers were trained in this way to imagine that they were part of the bow, arrow, and target. For self-defense, you, your weapon, and your target person become as one—you almost automatically go through the motions of ready, aim, fire. The bottom line is, your weapon is an extension of yourself. It is as if the chemical spray is built into your own body. Practice, physically and mentally, will increase your immediate readiness to react to a criminal and also make it possible for this mystic bonding of you, your weapon, and your target.

Of course, you can still be very proficient without this Zen meditative awareness. What's important is to become so skilled that when confronted, your personal internal alarm system sets off a smooth, deliberate response. The only way to achieve this is to carry your personal security devices with you, look and reflect on them regularly, and maintain alert status wherever you are with a personal radar scan that regularly asks "what if." Flying private planes is a pleasant pastime for many, but they are taught to exert the same kind of awareness in the event they have to make an emergency landing. Flying is still a pleasant experience, but with "personal radar scanning" it is also a *safe* pastime. The same is true for you and your personal security wherever you are.

The motto of the Coast Guard is *semper paratus*—"always ready." The same applies to you. What if both arms are used carrying bags, or only one hand is available to you and you are attacked? What if your chemical spray malfunctions or you miss? What if the assailant has closed in on you and you cannot escape (always the first choice)? You can use the spray can itself as a weapon, grasped firmly in your dominant hand, striking the assailant in the eye. You can kick your assailant in the shins. A knee to the groin may not be wise, because to land such a blow forcefully you have to be closer to the assailant than would be needed for a chemical spray defense and you could put yourself off balance.

Versatility is another skill to develop. Carrying more than one security device (but not too many), combining several techniques in the same situation, and having alternatives for similar situations are ways of being versatile. For example, as you use any security device you can scream or yell as loud as you can and kick the assailant's shins before backing off. If you were an assailant expecting a quick robbery or rape fantasy, how would you react to a yelling, screaming, kicking, clawing victim? It's like trying to corner a wildcat! This *versatile* defense increases the impact of your actions on the assailant and adds a psychological-emotional dimension. You should find a private place to practice unearthly, blood-curdling screams or a constant, machine-gun delivery of yelling ("No!") at peak lung power. This and short, powerful kicks to the shins added to proficient use of security devices should be your standard self-defense behavior.

While you can't overprepare to resist crime you can become overconfident. The danger in that is that you will not put escape first in your mind but will consider fighting back when the odds are even or against you. Worse still, you may take the law into your own hands and not only stand and fight but remain "to teach him/her a lesson." It is at that point that you are no longer a crime victim but a vigilante. Charles Bronson could do it in the *Death Wish* movie series, but in real life you will have to defend your actions just as criminals have to defend theirs. Justice and retribution are a court concern. Besides, you can get yourself permanently disabled or killed.

USEFUL RESOURCES

Though you may not support their strong advocacy for the right to bear arms, the National Rifle Association (NRA) is a good resource for information and publications on gun safety. The NRA also sponsors firearms courses and matches and uses good firing range standards.

Gun manufacturers sponsor amateur civilian and law enforcement matches with prizes of cash or guns. Only unaltered guns of the manufacturer are allowed. One such organization is the Glock Sport Shooting Foundation, P.O. Box 1254, Smyrna, GA 30081. Inquire at a major sporting goods store.

Pro-Tech Inc., P.O. Box 18235, Richmond, VA 23226 (phone: 804-358-6005) is a firm that field-tests and sells reliable personal security devices at reasonable cost.

Further Reading

Arif, A., & Westermeyer, J. (1988). *Manual of Drug and Alcohol Abuse*. New York: Plenum.

Black, H. C. (1979). *Black's Law Dictionary*. St. Paul, MN: West.

MacHovec, F. J. (1989). *Interview and Interrogation: A Scientific Approach*. Springfield, IL: Charles C. Thomas.

MacHovec, F. J. (1989). *Cults and Personality*. Springfield, IL: Charles C. Thomas.

MacHovec, F. J. (1992). *Security Services, Security Science*. Springfield, IL: Charles C. Thomas.

CHAPTER 3

Street Crime

THE FOUR Ds

Newspaper and TV crime reports prove you don't have to be looking for trouble to be immersed in it. Minding your own business is no guarantee criminals will not make *your* business *theirs*. You can become a victim suddenly, anywhere. Street crime involves four Ds:

1. *Distraction*. Either you are distracted and preoccupied or the criminal distracts you with some ploy.

2. *Deception*. Few crimes happen "straight on." Carjacking can follow being bumped from behind by the criminal's accomplice. The Boston Strangler posed as a repair man. Ted Bundy wore a fake cast on his arm and asked victims to help him to his car.

3. *Destruction*, of property or you, the crime itself.

4. *Deterrence*, the weak link in the chain of crime

prevention and the goal of this book. Deterrence includes avoiding high-risk situations, employing preventive practices when you're at risk, and taking the most appropriate action to escape unharmed.

To be street smart you need to know and understand typical street crimes, what they are, and where and how they happen.

WALKING AND JOGGING

The brutal attack of a woman jogging in Central Park shocked the conscience of many people and deterred them from venturing out into parks and roadways to walk and jog. Criminals, like predatory animals, look for the weak and vulnerable. What you say and do can increase your victim potential: being distracted or preoccupied, lost or uncertain, frail or passive. Wearing expensive clothing or jewelry suggests you're carrying a large amount of cash. If certain routine precautions are taken, walking and jogging can be safer:

1. Know where you walk and jog, where and how far to get help along the way.

2. Avoid any place where someone can hide.

3. Have someone with you if possible.

4. Carry some defensive weapon—at least a whistle or screecher, preferably pepper spray—and know how to use it.

5. Tell someone where you're going and how long you'll be.

6. Vary the time you walk or jog to deter stalkers or criminals who study your behavior pattern.

7. Beware of Walkman-type portable headsets. They can distract you and deafen you to anyone trying to warn you or the approach of a car or an assailant.

8. Wear a fanny pack—up front. Shoulders have been

dislocated when over-the-shoulder purses were forcibly taken.

9. Keep both hands free or carry a screecher or spray in one hand. If your hands are stuffed into a jacket or full of packages, there is no way you can defend yourself.

10. Dress for a fast escape. Jeans and sneakers are better than long coats and dresses. In rape situations, clothes that are difficult to remove give you a few more seconds to consider what you might do to escape.

Criminals avoid people who are aware of their surroundings and not likely to be surprised or caught off guard. Surprise is one of a criminal's most effective techniques. You can use it, too, in self-defense, such as by forcefully swinging a large shoulder bag into the criminal's face and then making a speedy escape to safety.

STALKERS

One of the most upsetting experiences is being stalked by someone who might harm you. Many entertainers have this problem. A fan becomes obsessed or fixated on them and writes, phones, attends repeat performances, and follows them from city to city. Through *paranoid erotomania*, a person can become psychologically and emotionally attached to you without any encouragement on your part. To the stalker it is a total investment—pure, absolute love. You close the draperies of your bedroom and see a form in the shadows across the street. On the way to work, school, shopping, even to and from church or temple that same person is close by. It can be someone you know or a stranger. Sooner or later, stalkers make their feelings known in letters, notes, gifts, phone calls, or in person. If you're nice to them they interpret it as acceptance. If you're nasty they see it as playing "hard to get" or testing their love for you. Being friendly or nasty doesn't deter them. It can be pretty scary. Tragically, stalkers have sometimes killed the person who is the object of their fixation. John Lennon was shot and killed by such a person.

Until recently, no laws prohibited stalking. More states are enacting laws to prevent it. Lawyers defending stalkers cite the First, Fourth, and Fifth Amendments, which ensure a person's freedom of movement. After all, you haven't been assaulted—yet. And there are some malicious people who might use anti-stalker laws to get back at a former lover or ex-spouse. Ideally, the police should be able to see the stalker in action. That proves the basis of your complaint. Consult a lawyer, too, to explore the possibility of a "peace bond" or restraining order that tightens restrictions on stalkers, who can be arrested if they make contact with you. If such a person touches you, you can charge them with assault, though this has not been an effective deterrent.

SERIAL KILLERS

Serial killers are even more terrifying than stalkers. Most of them have a deep need and strong drive to take captives, torture, rape, and kill, and they regularly repeat their crimes. They move frequently from job to job or across states and sometimes countries, making it difficult to track and catch them. They tend to target victims that in some way resemble someone in their past or in their fantasies. England's Jack the Ripper found White Hall hookers easy prey. We can only speculate as to the motive for the series of vicious murders. Ted Bundy's victims resembled a woman who rejected him years before. Jeffrey Dahmer preferred male teenagers. Albert DeSalvo, the "Boston Strangler," wanted sex four or more times a day and victimized any available female. It is estimated there are fifty serial killers loose in the United States at any time, about one per state.

Most serial killers convicted to date have been male

caucasians. African-American male and caucasian female serial killers are rare.

Based on statistical base rates, the typical serial killer is a male caucasian, twenty-five to thirty-five years old, who picks up victims close to his home comfort zone and transports them to a selected killing ground. Strangely, he is likely to return to the crime scene and sit and talk to the corpse. Victims are usually the same race as the killer. More experienced sex murderers carry a "rape kit," usually a weapon (gun or knife), mask, rope, duct tape, or even police handcuffs. Less experienced killers use weapons available on the scene or their own hands. Most serial killers are trophy hunters and like to take and keep a souvenir from victims such as a photo, jewelry, or a garment. As children, most serial killers never really bonded closely with anyone or anything, human or animal. Cruelty to animals is common. Many were bedwetters and fire setters. As adults they change jobs and move frequently, making no lasting friendships and having no long-term plans. They can have good social skills like Ted Bundy, or be eccentric loners like Jeffrey Dahmer.

What can you do to lessen your risk of being a serial killer's victim? Develop a more skeptical attitude toward anyone who "comes on" to you with a line that seems like a ruse or ploy. This is difficult but there are ways to keep a distance yet not reject good guys. If you slow down the socializing process, a potential killer is more likely to move on to another target. Be especially sensitive to anyone who wants to move you away from a public area or into his car or van. The next stop may be his killing ground. You can stall by arranging to meet another day or evening and in a public place. This gives you time to check him out. If dating someone you don't know well, someone new to town or to the job, keep the first few dates short, in safe places, and tell a friend where you'll be and the name and description of the person you'll be with.

AUTOMATIC TELLER MACHINES

The automatic teller machine (ATM) is considered a great convenience, and it is. It makes cash available any time of day or night to consumers—and criminals. It's best not to use them unless you really have to. Remember our golden rule: The best way to avoid being a crime victim is by *not being there*. If you must use an ATM, exercise these standard precautions *every* time:

1. Survey the scene as you arrive and before you leave your car or approach the ATM. If there is anyone there, wait for them to leave. The kindly old gentleman there may be a professional crook. A couple may be today's Bonnie and Clyde. Avoid using the ATM if it is in an isolated spot and there are shrubs or shadows that can conceal thieves.

2. If someone arrives after you have begun your transaction, move in close to the ATM and block the potential thief's vision over your shoulder. Thieves are after the ID numbers you punch in and try to get them directly or from a distance with binoculars or telephoto or zoom lenses on videotape and still cameras. Any "tourists" in the area when you are at the ATM should be viewed with suspicion. If you are in a wheelchair, take special precautions such as having a friend stand behind you.

3. Get in and out of there as soon as possible. It is a high-risk situation.

4. Save your receipt; *never* throw it away at or near the ATM. Many receipts list your ID number. Even if the number is coded, clever crooks may know how to decipher it.

5. Never put your ID number on the signature strip of your bank card. If you lose the card, thieves have easy access to your money.

Though it may seem far-fetched, uniformed crooks in Hartford, Connecticut, installed a state-of-the-art ATM in a busy shopping mall. It didn't pay out any money but notified customers there was a computer problem. All ID numbers entered were screened on a lap-top computer connected to the ATM and located a short distance away. The thieves gained access to scores of account numbers before the plot was discovered. There is no protection against this kind of sophisticated crime, though bank officials quickly increased security measures to prevent this practice.

Automatic teller cash dispensers have been improved. There is now a "cashlock system," an enclosure much like a phone booth. The door opens electronically only when you insert a correct bank card. It closes automatically to protect you while you transact your business, then opens when you push a button inside. One consolation to ATM theft is that you are usually liable only for the first fifty dollars stolen.

BANKS

Despite sophisticated state-of-the-art internal and external security, bank robberies still occur, though more money is stolen internally by bank officers and employees. Since the days of Jesse James and Bonnie and Clyde, bank robberies have been dramatic and terrifying crimes. There are a dozen bank robberies a day in Los Angeles. Few bank robberies are well planned. The vast majority of robbers are apprehended and they average only three thousand dollars per robbery. There is a risk of hostage taking if the thief's escape route is blocked.

It's good preventive practice to observe a bank as you approach it, first from your car, then as you walk toward it. Watch for suspicious characters such as anyone with a hat over their eyes, wearing sunglasses, carrying an empty bag, wearing baggy clothing or a bulge that could be a gun, and with a car at the curb. You may feel foolish, but pausing a few minutes or doing another chore to delay going into the bank won't cost you anything, and it could save you from a traumatic psychological event.

A New Zealand firm has developed an automated bank robber detector. It combines several state-of-the-art sensing devices in an integrated computerized system. A metal detector checks for metal density matching that of a gun, electronic sensors measure heart rate and speed of footsteps, and a video camera is triggered by a face reflecting low light such as when a mask or hood is worn or a hat is turned down to obscure the face. When all these factors are positive, a silent alarm is activated to bank staff and the bank entry door closes, locking the suspect outside the bank, which is filmed by a security camera. The cost of this system is less than for a full-time security guard.

CREDIT CARD FRAUD

Take extra care with your credit cards. Do not give anyone your credit card ID numbers by phone, mail, or in person unless you know you are dealing with an established firm.

CAR CRIME

There are many kinds of car crime. Your car can be stolen just about anywhere: at home, at work, while shopping, visiting friends, or on vacation. It can happen when you are not there or as you approach, enter, or leave it, and even while driving (as in carjacking). Motives of car thieves vary from teenage joy riders to drug dealers who need a car temporarily and "chop shops" that dismantle cars for twice the car's value in spare parts. Joy riders can break into your car in less than a minute, and chop shops can reduce your car to unrecognizable parts in less than ten minutes. Most people are not aware of how easy it is to be the victim of car crime. Commonsense precautions will greatly reduce the probability. What is your safety IQ *right now*? To find out, on a separate piece of paper note your honest response to these twenty yes-or-no questions:

Street Smart Driver Test

1. I always lock my car when I leave it, wherever I am.

2. I never pick up strangers, even if they are of the same sex and look friendly.

3. I never get in a stranger's car, even for help.

4. I never leave bags, parcels, boxes, briefcases, luggage, or valuables within view anywhere in the car.

5. I always carry a whistle, sound device, or chemical spray and hold it firmly in my dominant hand when approaching or leaving my car.

6. I always park in a carefully chosen safe location on the street, parking lot, or garage with more than one escape route and easy access for help.

7. I never roll down the window more than an inch to talk to anyone, even police officers.

8. I am always aware of what and who is in, near, in front of, behind, and under my car as I approach it.

9. I have a metal flashlight to light up dark garages that can also be used by me as a weapon.

10. If my car is a two-door I always set front car seats forward so I can see anyone concealed in the back.

11. I always plan my driving for maximum daylight and avoid high-crime areas and unfamiliar areas.

12. I always note the license number of any suspicious vehicle.

13. I know where the hazard light control is in my car and could find and operate it in the dark.

14. If my car is disabled I always stay with it and do not hitchhike, walk for help, or stand outside.

15. I never leave my car for a stranger who offers to help me.

16. I always ask police—uniformed or plainclothes—for ID and I know what proper ID looks like.

17. I always keep my car serviced and in good repair.

18. I always scan wherever I am for the best and safest escape.

19. I have flares or reflectors and know how to use them.

20. I have a CB radio or cellular phone in my car.

Score five points for every *yes* answer, and subtract five points for *no* answers. The most security-conscious person scores 100, with no *no* answers. Your score is your safety IQ or how much you place yourself at risk. Look over the questions again. They are guidelines for your safety and security. Please take action to raise your safety IQ.

Some states have HEAT programs (Help Eliminate Auto Theft), funded by insurance firms and operated by police and motor vehicle licensing authorities. They are clearing houses for public and police information, operate hotlines, offer rewards for tips on chop shops and theft rings, and conduct public awareness programs to increase consumer awareness of the realities of auto theft. If there is no HEAT program in your state, you may want to help promote one.

Joy rider thieves are usually teenagers, most of whom are too young to be licensed drivers. They usually break the driver's side window, open the door, break the steering column housing, and try to hot-wire the ignition with a screw driver. Valuables are stolen from cars by breaking any window then opening a door. Chop shops seek cars for their parts. More sophisticated car thieves steal for resale out of state or overseas. Legal titles are obtained from wrecked cars then transferred to stolen cars of the same make and model. Drug dealers and "mules" (transporters) sometimes use stolen cars. If things go wrong they leave the car, which cannot be traced to them personally.

To and From Your Car

As stressed throughout this book, the best protection against crime is not to be in or near a crime situation. In terms of your car, the best preventive is to be aware of where you are, the place and the people there, the relative risk potential, and anything that would make the situation appealing to criminals. The goal is to develop an automatic *yes* to all twenty of the questions in the above quiz.

Always visually scan your car and anything and anyone near it as you approach it. If anything looks suspicious, pretend to have forgotten something, turn, and go back where it is safe until the situation is more secure. If in doubt, *get out of there*. Show a confident, aware manner by walking purposefully, looking alert, in control, and able to take care of yourself. Have pepper spray firmly gripped in your dominant hand, thumb at the ready on the firing button. Unlock and enter your car quickly, being sure the area is clear of loiterers or passers by, and lock yourself in promptly.

Parking

Always think ahead *where* you will park—the immediate area, nearest stores, banks, and phone. Park in busy, well-lighted areas away from shadows, pillars, and doorways where someone can hide, and close to exits, elevators, streets, or toll booths. Do not rely on closed-circuit TV cameras—they may not be on, just dummy units, or the security officer could be asleep or making rounds. Drive around in parking lots and garages, looking for anyone crouched between or behind cars, or suspicious people just hanging around.

If you drive a two-door, always put the seats forward when you park so you can see anyone hiding in the back. Make it a habit to drive with the passenger seat forward so you won't have to get out of the car to do this after you park, increasing your exposure time to an assailant. This also prevents or at least delays persons forcing themselves into your car from the passenger side.

Other tips: have a large metal flashlight in your car. Use it to check out darkened areas and as a weapon if you need it. Also, a backhanded punch to the eyes is quicker to deliver than a "roundhouse" blow to the head and will disable the criminal longer.

The Stopped Car

A common ploy of criminals is to throw a rock or bottle against your car when you are stopped at a traffic light or stop sign. When you get out of the car you are attacked or robbed or your car is stolen. If your car is struck by an object and you do not know the cause *do not get out of the car* but quickly drive off to a well-lighted public area and *then* get out to look. If you are confronted with assailants while stopped, honk the horn in quick, short blasts as you drive off. If you are certain it is a criminal attack and have a reasonable concern that your life is in danger, drive on even if the assailant is standing in front of the car.

The Moving Car

Some carjackers and rapists have signalled motorists along the highway or on the street as if there was a flat or something wrong with the victim's car. If this ever happens, smile and drive on to the next exit, gas station, or public area and check it out. Avoid rest stops—the assailant may be following you and there may be no one there to help. Drive into well-lighted, open, public areas. While you may think it rude, it is best to ask even a uniformed police officer for ID and *look at it*. Better to be safe than sorry. Know the uniforms, cars, license tag style, and ID of your local and state police. Next time you see a local or state police officer, ask him or her about these. Blame this book if it makes it less embarrassing to you! Tell someone you know and trust your travel plan, dates, route, and estimated times of arrival and departure. They may think you're paranoid, but you have nothing to lose but your life! *Never* pick up strangers. Know your car, how it handles, quickest start and getaway, braking, and turning circle. *Never* pick up a hitchhiker.

If for any reason you are frightened for your safety while driving, put your hazard lights on to attract attention, maintain control of your car, and drive to the nearest police or fire station or well-lighted public place, and stop there to regain your composure.

Being Followed

If you are followed or think you are being followed, *never* drive home. Drive to the nearest police station, park as close to it as possible, and hail the next officer you see. Do not get out of the car. Observe the person and vehicle who followed you. Note the person's appearance details (age, race, height, weight, distinguishing features), the make and color of car, and the license number. In most cases, this is enough to discourage anyone following you. The worst that can happen is the police think you're hypersensitive. If there is no police station nearby, drive to the nearest busy, well-lit public place.

Look for a police officer. If there is no other way, leave your car quickly, go to a phone, and dial the authorities. A cellular phone in your car is a very good and reliable security device.

Police Imposters

One motorist who pulled off the road in response to a flashing light on the dash of a car following him was robbed at gunpoint by a police imposter. There is a growing number of carjackings, rapes, and murders by criminals impersonating uniformed and plainclothes police and security officers. You should know some basic police traffic procedures. Generally, plainclothes officers are not on traffic duty. Blue flashing lights are used by police, red for firetrucks, and amber for towing vehicles, but all of these lights are available to private citizens through auto accessory stores. Familiarize yourself with the color and style of city, county, and state police uniforms, their cars, badges, and standard equipment. It's helpful to have their phone numbers as well—a cellular phone in the car enables you to verify an officer's ID. If it's a crook, he'll take off like the proverbial bat out of hell. If that happens, be sure to get his license number.

You are legally required to stop if requested to do so by a police officer. Pull off the road in a well-lighted area or where there are others present who can witness what is happening. It's worth the embarrassment or anxiety to prevent a phony cop from stopping you. If there is no safe stopping place nearby, reduce speed slightly, wave, then point forward so the officer knows you're not ignoring the request. If the officer seems irritated when you finally talk with him or her, explain the situation. Open your window only an inch so that you can talk with the officer and slip ID through the narrow opening. You are required to show police officers your driver's license, vehicle registration, and in some areas, proof of insurance. Always take your license out of your wallet to avoid suspicion of bribery. Keep your hands on the steering wheel or in plain sight. Police are sensitive about possible concealed weapons. You have a Fourth Amendment right against unreasonable search and seizure, which is overruled if an officer has "probable cause"—reason to believe there are illegal or stolen goods in the vehicle.

If you are suspicious or not entirely certain you are faced with a legitimate police officer, you can ask for ID. Look at it closely enough so you can describe it if it turns out to be fake. It can help apprehend the imposter. If you feel embarrassed asking for ID, blame this book! But if ever in doubt about police or security officer identity, *ask*. Consult an attorney or the police internal affairs unit later if you feel the officer has been unreasonable.

Car Breakdowns

If ever your car breaks down, attach a white handkerchief to the antenna, the most visible door handle, or atop the driver's window and *stay with the car*. Never, ever roll down the window or get out of the car if a stranger approaches and offers help. Do not trust individuals, couples, or families. *Never* go in a stranger's car for help. If someone offers to come and help you, *discourage them* and ask them to phone for help. Roll the window down an inch and offer a quarter for the call. Motorists in distress have been attacked and robbed by criminals who used CB radio to locate them. Carry flares or reflectors and know how to use them. If you must get out of the car, carry a metal flashlight that can be used as a club, or have your chemical spray handy. Check flashlight batteries regularly.

• • •

Gas Stations and Convenience Stores

Gas stations and convenience stores are choice targets for armed robbers, especially during off-hours when there are few people around. Avoid being there at such times. Whenever you drive into a gas station, choose a pump that is well-lighted and nearest the store or pay station. You may not be able to make your way to the booth if accosted, but chances are the clerk there can see what's going on and quickly report it, and others there can come to your aid. If you are in a convenience store that is being robbed, *do not be a hero.* Avoid eye contact but notice as much as you can about the robber by indirect side glances. Do not try to reason with him or her and *never* argue. If he or she tells you to drop to the floor, do so at once, facing down. Staring at an assailant can increase his or her anxiety, and triggers have been pulled by a nervous twitch. Cooperate with police later, telling them everything you remember, even if you feel it is an insignificant detail. Details from many persons provide a more complete description than any single informant.

Carjacking

Carjacking is motor vehicle theft by force. A driver is confronted by an assailant and forced to surrender the vehicle. Most law enforcement agencies classify carjacking as robbery or armed robbery—not theft, since the owner is present—and robbery carries heavier penalties than theft. Why carjack? There are several reasons:

1. Waiting for the driver to deactivate alarms and anti-theft devices makes stealing the car easier.
2. Gang initiation or rite of passage
3. Status symbol, macho image

4. Thrill of joyriding
5. Quick cash for the car or its parts
6. Media coverage makes it appealing

Most carjackings occur at night, in cities, towns, and rural areas. The target is the vehicle, not the driver. Guns are frequently used by carjackers, and drivers have been shot or injured in some cases even when passively submitting. Other weapons used by carjackers include knives, sticks, baseball bats, pipes, crowbars, long metal flashlights, and rocks. "Jackers" typically use one of three ploys:

1. The carjacker fakes a minor accident by bumping into your car from behind, or throwing a rock or bottle at it. When you get out to look at the damage a carjacker rushes in and drives off. In such a situation, you should not get out of your car unless there are other cars and people nearby. If no one else is there, wave to the other operator and signal him or her to follow you to the nearest public area. If he or she does not, note the license number, car make, and driver and passengers. Whenever you leave your vehicle, always look around, stay alert, and take your wallet and keys with you.

2. The carjacker approaches on foot while your car is stopped at a traffic light, stop sign, road work area, or parked at a gas station, car wash, automatic teller machine, or convenience store.

3. The carjacker approaches from cover in a shopping mall, parking lot, garage, or rest stop as the victim enters or leaves vehicle, or at highway entrance or exit ramps as the vehicle slows or stops.

When you leave your car to investigate or converse you are attacked or confronted with a weapon, usually a gun. If this happens, surrender your keys, back off, and run away.

The pecking order is simple: a gun outranks your kubotan or chemical spray. Even if you're very fast, a nervous crook can shoot you in a split second, and up close it's unlikely he'll miss. Instead, make mental notes of his or her appearance to help police search later. Practice by observing people as you walk and drive (age, gender, hair and eye color, clothing, distinguishing features).

Teen gangs and groups of rowdies like the risk and high of carjacking. They sometimes joy ride in several stolen or carjacked vehicles over one weekend, leaving them at the curb or abandoning them when they run out of gas. Drug runners carjack to use vehicles along the interstate highway system. Thieves in the Miami area rob and sometimes kill foreign tourists who wander lost on their way from the airport to the city. In New York, Los Angeles, and other big cities up to a dozen cars are stolen every day. Sporty or late model cars are not necessarily those most stolen. Many thieves like cars that are less conspicuous such as intermediate-sized sedans more than five years old. And older cars may be more valuable for their hard-to-find parts.

The best safeguard against carjacking is *always* following routine preventive practice such as avoiding high-crime, dimly lit, and isolated areas away from people or phones. If you must be in such areas, do not go there alone. Some other security guidelines:

1. Always walk directly to and from your car, keys firmly in hand, remaining alert. Look around and inside your car before entering.

2. Always lock yourself inside, all windows up or only one-inch of air space (un-air conditioned discomfort is better than being hurt or killed). If you feel uneasy, even if you don't know why, get in and quickly drive away.

3. Avoid driving alone, especially at night and in areas

unfamiliar to you. Know the area well, exactly where you are at all times—main and alternate routes, dead ends, detours, and construction sites.

4. Know where there are police and fire stations, public phones, hospitals, gas stations, open stores, and friends' homes along the route, just in case.

5. If *anyone* (even a uniformed police or security officer) approaches, open the window *only an inch*. Ask for ID and know what correct ID looks like. Be suspicious if asked out of the car for no apparent good reason. If you feel uneasy, ask the officer to request backup. If other officers show up, you know the first one is legitimate. Serial killers *have* posed as police and security officers.

6. Stay in open, clear lanes and scan escape routes as you drive, just in case. In a carjack situation when it is obvious you are in danger or are being attacked, drive through a red traffic light or off the street over unobstructed open space. It is better to risk a moving traffic violation than injury or death.

7. Always allow one car length between your vehicle and others, to give you maneuvering room if you need to pull out of the lane and escape. Drive in center lanes to avoid carjackers walking or running up to your car.

8. Never have valuables, bags, packages, briefcases, or luggage in plain view. "Big boom" speakers strongly tempt teenage carjackers.

9. Never leave your keys in the ignition when you are not in the vehicle.

10. Park and lock. Park in well-lit public areas and always lock your car whenever and wherever you leave it. Garages with attendants are preferred. Leave only the ignition key—no house keys or address ID. High-risk locations include near dumpsters, trees or shrubs, trucks or vans, and unlighted areas.

11. If you see a theft or carjacking in progress, report it immediately and observe what is happening so you can describe it to police and help apprehend the culprits. Don't stop to help strangers; drive to the nearest gas station or phone. Report all crimes immediately.

12. Keep your vehicle registration *with you*, not in the vehicle. Keep house and car keys separate. Keep your car serviced, in good running order, with gas tank full or nearly so (water condenses in empty tanks). A CB radio (good) or cellular phone (better) can link you to help. Be aware that some people have been victimized by crooks who answered the CB call. A telephone call to authorities is safer.

Here are some foolish mistakes some drivers make that are special invitations to car thieves:

1. Leaving car unlocked or with the keys inside, in isolated or dimly lit locations.

2. Starting the car in the morning and leaving it idling while finishing breakfast.

3. Leaving keys in the car at convenience store, gas station, car dealer, or outside a car wash.

4. Putting a spare key in a magnetic tin inside front or rear bumpers—often the first place a thief looks. A better place is in your wallet or purse, with you when it's needed.

5. Getting into and out of a car while distracted or inattentive.

Another form of carjacking is to test drive a car from a dealer or owner then drive off into the sunset.

Buying a Stolen Car

"Who, me?" you might ask in shock or disbelief. Yes,

you! If you buy a used car, *be suspicious* if:

1. It's a late model car with a new paint job.
2. Keys are not the original manufacturer's keys.
3. It's at a bargain price. If it's too good to be true, maybe it isn't so good.
4. There is anything unusual about the car's title, identification number, or ID tag.

Thieves disposing of stolen cars often use newspaper ads, supermarket and community bulletin boards, word of mouth, or street conversations. Chop shops often operate in salvage yards, especially at new and different locations. If someone offers you a hard-to-get part immediately, cheap, and for cash, be suspicious. When you buy a used car, use the same care as you would buying a house: check the title. Every car has an ID number, usually at or near the fire wall separating the engine compartment from the passenger area. That number should be on the title. Be suspicious if the number strip has been screwed or glued on or looks new. It could be the ID of a wrecked car replacing that of a stolen car. It's a good idea to mark your own car in several inconspicuous places by dropping your business card down the windshield area or between windows. This can identify your vehicle if stolen and ID numerals are changed.

Vehicle Anti-Theft Devices

There are several products that can slow down and discourage car thieves:

Wheel clubs are heavy metal rods that key-lock onto the steering wheel so the wheel cannot be turned fully left or right. If a thief wants the vehicle badly enough and has time, he or she can use a spray can of freezer mist to freeze and shatter the lock mechanism. Wheel clubs are better than nothing and slow down thieves. If the thief has two vehicles side by side to choose from, the one without the wheel club is most likely to be stolen. Wheel clubs cost about fifty dollars.

Car alarms can flash headlights and sound the horn if the vehicle is broken into. Unfortunately, they can malfunction and go off when there is no theft or fail when there is. There are many vehicle security alarm systems to choose from. Buy a good one from a reliable firm and test it monthly. They cost $60 to $100 if you install them yourself, $100 to $500 if professionally installed. Good economy units are Audiovox AA-9200 or Whistler 525; better units are the Audiovox AA-9247 or AA-9127; and the most sophisticated are Audiovox TSP-550, TSP-750, or Whistler 536. Some systems are portable and can easily be moved from one vehicle to another. Most have LED "on" lights and a valet switch that disengage the systems for parking lots. Features currently available:

- adjustable shock sensor for break-ins
- remote control that activates the system from a keyring micro-transmitter
- remote panic alarm which, once activated, sounds a siren or the car horn and automatically resets and repeats until you disable it—handy if you're disabled or overpowered
- voltage drop sensor that activates the alarm if inside dome or trunk light goes on
- arm-disarm sensor that sounds alarm if the system is turned on or off by anyone but you
- motion detector that sounds alarm if the vehicle is moved, towed, or jacked up
- remote control door lock and unlock starter disabler that makes it impossible to start the car
- four-watt transmitter pager, the same power output of a CB transmitter, that signals you, aloud or by silent alarm, within a mile of the vehicle

"ARM" Yourself

Whenever you are behind the wheel, ARM yourself!

A stands for *anticipate* and also being *alert, aware, attentive, able.* Be a people watcher, noting especially wandering gangs of teenagers, circling or moving toward you. Troubled youth in gangs are uninhibited and more prone to violence. Remember the Central Park jogger who was brutally raped by teenagers who were "wilding?" Start a "what if" mental scan of alternatives the moment you see potential assailants, such as: where am I, where can I go now, what help is closest, is there enough room to drive away, etc. Look up and out, vigilant but not vulnerable, able to resist if you choose to do so, and not passive and submissive with averted, fearful eyes. Learn to stare them down as your body maintains readiness to drive away. Practice in a mirror. *Always* keep your seatbelt fastened firmly, as you do in airliners. *Know your car*, how to start from a standing stop fast without spinning wheels, turn in tight corners, brake hard without losing control. *Maintain your car.* Have it serviced regularly. Stalling out in a crisis can cost you your life.

R stands for *react* and *rehearse.* Practice quick starts and tight turns on large, empty parking lots on Sundays, holidays, or after hours. Be prepared to explain what you are doing to any curious police—blame this book! You should feel part of your car and that your car is an extension of yourself.

M stands for *moving* or *maneuvering,* driving decisively and defensively, with deliberate action, safely and purposefully out of danger. Never drive into a one-way street the wrong way unless you can see clearly that no other vehicles are coming. Jump the curb only if there's no other way to escape. You can drive on a flat tire out of danger if your life depends on it, but it will slow you down and increase the risk of losing control.

Steer Clear of Emergency Vehicles

There is an increase in scofflaws who do not pull over to give the right of way to ambulances or emergency vehicles. In some cases there have been serious accidents and those in the ambulance or those waiting for the ambulance have died. When you see flashing lights anywhere, exercise caution, pull over, or stop to let them pass. The life you save may be someone you know. Some day it may be you.

SHOPPING

Shopping can still be fun if you are a *defensive shopper*. Always park in the most well-lighted, heavily trafficked spot, not at the edge of lots where there can be bushes, trees, and poor lighting—ideal for thieves and rapists. If there are other shoppers approaching the store, walk with them. Do not, however, walk alone with an individual who looks suspicious, or even if he or she does not. Arms full of packages and small children at your side are a special invitation to thieves. Whenever possible use a buddy system, another person who can stand in safety on the pavement or a store doorway while you park and later as you return to the car. Arrive earlier when there are parking spaces closer to well-lit, safe areas. Remember, most criminals don't look like criminals.

HOSTAGE SITUATIONS AND TERRORISM

The 1993 bombing of the World Trade Center in downtown New York proves beyond any doubt that terrorists can strike anywhere they want if they really want to. Hostages have been taken in stores, shopping malls, restaurants, and hotels—even in court and in prison. You are not immune from either of these frightening situations. Knowing what to expect can help reduce your anxiety about these traumatic events and help you cope with them if they ever occur.

Being taken hostage is a high-stress, high-risk situation for physical and psychological harm. Hostage taking can be carefully planned, a sudden impulse, or part of a felon's panic reaction. Generally, risk to hostages rises with the impulse or panic level of hostage takers. Guns have gone off simply by a nervous twitch of the trigger finger. Experts say the first hour is the most dangerous, because the situation is unstable. The hostage-takers are not familiar with the room and building, details inside and outside the area, and do not know what's happening or being planned outside. If you are a hostage you can increase danger by resisting, arguing, or trying to influence your captors. Do not stare at them. It is important that you know how hostage situations are handled so that you don't interfere with the process or put yourself and others in danger.

Local, state, and federal law enforcement officers are well trained in hostage negotiation. They know more than you and they are outside with all the resources needed to end the situation. As time passes the advantage passes to the police and toward peaceful resolution. The surrounding area will be cleared as much as possible and one phone line will be reserved for police–captor communication with one contact person on either side. In some cases a hostage has been the captor's choice contact. If you are that person, do only as you're told, be an open channel, and do not try to manipulate either side. You will be under stress and your judgment may be impaired. You will not know or fully understand what is being planned by both sides, the realities, or potential danger. Be a good listener if hostage takers vent feelings or explain their reasons for creating the situation. Be aware, though, that the longer you are a captive the more likely you will develop a sympathy for your captors. This is called the

"Stockholm syndrome" after researchers in that city who first described it. When the situation ends you will be "debriefed" by police as to what happened. It's okay to be upset.

Police negotiators will exert every effort to keep messages clear and simple to minimize misunderstanding, build trust, and eliminate surprises. Third parties such as lawyers, friends, family, and news reporters will be urged to go through this single police–captor communications link. If they do not they weaken and can confuse negotiations. The police contact will offer to trade captors for food, money, or messages to media or government officials. Police negotiators gradually become benefactors providing food and a safer, more stable environment. Hopefully the idea surfaces that surrender without harm to captors or hostages is the fairest, most logical end. Trained negotiators will not lie or threaten captors in the hope that this sense of fairness will spread into the captor–captive situation. This did not happen in the Waco Branch Davidian case. There the cult leader David Koresh consistently refused to cooperate or keep promises, ending in the tragic deaths of men, women, and children cult members.

SCAMS, RIPOFFS, STINGS

In his book *Hidden Persuaders*, Vance Packard listed eight "psychological hooks" used by advertisers—and con artists—to defraud you of your money:

- emotional security
- ego, image, status
- love, pleasure
- creative outlet
- self-worth
- power, money
- roots

- immortality

To that list I would add loneliness, quest for meaning, and the universal need for acceptance, belonging, and personal and emotional support. Most people are vulnerable to one or more of these "hooks." Clever crooks use more than one. They are used not only by con artists but also unscrupulous politicians, phony religions and cults, and by some personal growth and psychotherapy gurus. The antidote is critical thinking, a basic skepticism, and resisting any and all these "hooks" until the good faith of the person and the movement is clear. It helps to share your concerns with trusted friends and consult with professionals in the field or other knowledgeable people. David Koresh in Waco and Jim Jones in Guyana would never have had a following if everyone involved exercised more caution. As the Bible says, "By their fruits you shall know them." The Koresh and Jones trees produced only pain and violence—bitter fruit. Don't be hooked by those eight built-in traps.

The silver bullet of protection against scams and ripoffs is this rule: If it seems too good to be true, *it is*. Here's a parade of frequent scams:

Phony IRS agent. The phony agent calls and informs you that the IRS will withhold tax refunds and arrest you unless you pay up right away. The "agent" wants cash immediately or else. Ask for ID and phone number of their field office and call to check. The IRS hotline is 800-366-4484.

Phony IRS audit. This is a variation of the phony agent scam. In this case you are asked for your social security and credit card numbers.

Lucky winner. You are notified you've won a lottery you didn't even enter. But you have to pay taxes on your winnings—in cash, of course—before you can collect the grand prize.

Medical fraud. Unnecessary tests and examinations that can exceed two thousand dollars are not unusual. Sometimes there's a phony diagnosis so that unneeded treatment can be continued. In other cases, insurance carriers are billed for treatment that was never provided.

Models/actors agencies. Reputable firms do not charge cash fees to place you in a directory for jobs. They work on commission. Phony dating and escort services and model agencies are fronts for prostitution and pornography.

Charity. It is possible for private citizens to buy empty countertop space and free standing candy dispensers and collections containers. While most are legitimate, some have been found to be phony. Crooks maintain a collections route and pocket the money. Check with the National Charities Information Center if you suspect charity fraud.

Loan sharks. They are still around! They do business by mail or newspaper ads and offer loans up to $20,000, but you must send $250 cash with your application. Most are "boiler room" basement operations with multiple phone lines. They quickly close shop and move to another city as the law closes in. If the mail is used to defraud, it is a federal offense enforced by postal inspectors. If newspaper ads are used, local police "bunco squads" investigate and prosecute. One operation recently exposed raised $300,000 in one week from forty-three states.

Timeshare or campsite swindle. The swindler calls to inform you there is a buyer interested in your property and will be made known to you for a cash advance or finder's fee of several hundred dollars. Legitimate firms don't require money up front. Get the person's name, phone number, and ask for references. That's enough to deter crooks and shouldn't ruffle honest business people.

•　　　•　　　•

SAFE STREETS

You can help make streets safer and others street smart through the Safe Streets Initiative. Established by the FBI, it operates through task forces of local police and FBI field divisions. The goal is to help apprehend criminals involved in street violence (gangs, drug rings, bank robbers, kidnappers, contract murderers) and interstate theft (hijacking, carjacking, chop shops, fencing stolen goods). Regional task forces focus on the most frequent crimes in the immediate geographic area. In 1993 there were 85 task forces in 49 states. Some task forces have organized local community outreach programs such as the Red Hat Coalition (civilian patrols), Adopt-a-school (police and FBI talk with students), and Junior G-men (students are taught crime prevention). For more information about these programs contact your nearest FBI field office or phone 202-324-4245.

USEFUL RESOURCES

Bergeron, R. (1990). *Guard Against Attack In and Around Your Car.* Free booklet. Shell Oil Company, P.O. Box 4681, Houston, TX 77210.

National Center for Missing and Exploited Children. *KidCare ID* program (current child color photo and ID information). 1835 K Street NW, Suite 700, Washington, DC 20006.

National Crime Prevention Council, Distribution Section. Useful anti-carjacking kit, $9.95 prepaid. 1700 K Street NW, 2nd floor, Washington, DC 20906-3817.

CHAPTER 4

Work, School, and Vacation Crime

CRIME IN THE WORKPLACE

Since 1990 there have been over a hundred people killed while at work. Perpetrators are most often disgruntled employees or former employees who cannot cope with being terminated. They brood and obsess about it more than is normal or healthy. They feel they've lost everything. They became psychologically and emotionally overdependent on the job, unable to function normally without it. It was the central anchor in their life, and when it's suddenly taken from them they feel compelled to take drastic action to get it back or to get back. Typically, these violent reactors are socially withdrawn loners who blame others for their problems. Alcohol or drug abuse is common and lowers their behavior controls, which makes them more impulsive and unpredictable—human bombs waiting to go off. If they have excess self-pity, alcohol or drugs, and a weapon, these factors combine into a deadly mix of motive, means, and opportunity. If you are a manager, consider these rules to reduce risk of violence in the workplace:

1. Terminate employees at the end of their shift and the last day of the week. This minimizes their contact with others and the danger to themselves and others.

2. All terminated employees should have an exit interview by a personnel manager or person other than their immediate supervisor. This gives them the opportunity to safely vent feelings.

3. Terminated employees should be informed of counseling services in the firm or at the local mental health clinic. Tell them it's routine, not that you feel they need it, which can rub salt into their bleeding mental wound.

4. No terminated employee is allowed in their former office or work area. Security officers should strictly enforce this rule.

Violent crime can occur wherever you work: in an office, bank, store, restaurant, shopping mall, on the street, even in court, a post office, or a cemetery. All these places have been featured in major news events of crime in the workplace. Most of the perpetrators are disgruntled employees or those recently fired. The really bad news is that they might be no different than people who live in your neighborhood.

Some people invest their whole life in the job, and when it is taken from them they have great difficulty coping with the loss. It is overwhelming to them, especially when they do not understand or cannot accept the reason for their termination. This is so even when they have had serious problems on the job such as a genuine inability to do the work, sleeping on the job, theft, or when there has been alcoholism or drug abuse. They seldom see their own shortcomings. It is not unusual, then, for them to be paranoid about being criticized, corrected, or terminated. When that happens it has to be by "that SOB boss" or "the no-good coworker who took my job." As the person is left to brood over this loss, irritation and frustration become anger and rage. What to us might be "I'd like to go tell 'em off" becomes "I'm gonna kill 'em."

Daily news media—newspapers and television—offer abundant evidence of this destructive force. There has been an average of one shootout a year by a postal worker in a post office somewhere in the United States. A hospital orderly shot and killed his supervisor who legitimately charged him with excessive breaks and sleeping on the job. Desperate husbands have shot their estranged wives, their attorneys, and judges. Recall the tragic case of San Francisco's mayor Mosconi, shot by a prominent former city official and police officer.

While women make up almost half of the work force, violent employees or former employees are male. They are typically thirty- to forty-year-old loners, unmarried, and with few friends—no personal support system. The job is their only social contact. Many are a bit eccentric, don't mix well with others, and are the butt of office jokes. This can deepen their alienation and fester into rage that finally erupts in a killing spree. Interestingly, many of these social misfits change jobs or move away to lessen their own stress. But a lack of success in the next job again triggers the frustration-to-rage buildup. The work world is seen as unfair, unkind, and evil.

Some violent employees obsess over violent television programs and crime magazines. Alcohol or drug abuse potentiates pre-occupation with violence. Drugs remove inhibitions and depress. Purchasing a gun soon follows, a symbol of personal power and superiority that is seen as the one sure way to right all the wrongs finally and forever. Some perpetrators give signs of their intentions by word or action but because they are so socially isolated there's no one to notice or intervene. Here are some preventive actions you can take in the work place to reduce the risk of these violent incidents:

1. Establish a caring, friendly atmosphere, a team spirit of mutual support. Don't demean anyone.

2. Have an open-door policy for anyone who does not understand expected behavior, rules, policies, and procedures.

3. Allow a cooling-off period in a safe place with an experienced or trusted person for a reasonable time if an employee is agitated or upset. This vents negative emotions and provides a sympathetic ear, rather than bottling up more resentment.

4. Provide immediate support for anyone terminated or receiving a serious reprimand. Fire the last hour of the last day of the week. This lessens exposure to potential victims and an upsetting experience for other employees. An exit interview with a neutral person vents emotion and can provide clues of potential violence. Offer the interview but don't force it. If they accept, it's a good sign. If they don't, consider it a signal of increased risk potential.

5. Have all paperwork and final details in one place at one time to eliminate an employee going to car or locker. If the employee seems potentially dangerous, have a security officer escort him or her to and from the locker and car and ensure complete exit from building and grounds. Be sure all company ID and keys are returned. A termination checklist is helpful to satisfy these details.

6. *Never* allow a terminated employee to return to the workplace. This should be clearly stated to terminated employees *and* given to them in writing. Enforce this rule without exception. Someone fired Friday afternoon may show up over the weekend. If no one is working over the weekend, security should be bolstered.

Witnesses and surviving victims of violence in the workplace need the support of fellow workers, supervisors, and company executives, and counseling or therapy. It's worth the time and money. The best therapy for everyone is "family feeling" and "fellow feeling," a unified, strong sense of sharing together in the pain and stress, gradually growing into belonging and restored self-confidence. If this is not done, employees can get anxious or depressed, and productivity can decrease.

Internal and External Crime

White-collar crime in the workplace involves property (theft of product) or currency (cash, checks, credit), and you can be a suspect if you are anywhere near the offender. Security experts estimate that twenty million firms are using electronic surveillance by hidden camera or random or regular monitoring of computer databases and phone lines. Though controversial, these measures have been found appropriate by courts if limited to business and not personal communications. Your boss has an ethical and legal right to know what you are doing on the job.

Computer Crime

Computer use and abuse has introduced high-tech crime to the workplace. Estimates range from $1 billion to $200 billion in losses if you include indirect effects of deliberate computer misuse. Commercial and telecommunications firms are prime targets and loss is in money, information, or services. Most computer crime is internal, by employees. Outsiders account for less than a third of computer crimes.

Some of what is considered computer crime is human error. If you use a computer in your work, be aware your honest error can be misinterpreted as criminal intent. You can also be used by a "hacker" or computer criminal to provide information that can be used to commit computer crime. The antidote is to keep your supervisor informed of your mistakes and anyone asking for information not normally provided. Typical hackers have been bored, intelligent male Caucasians between seventeen and twenty-eight, usually nonconformist loners obsessed with computers. Their acts vary from implanting a virus or disrupting operations for fun, to show their superior expertise, malicious destruction of files, or to divert services, credit, or money to themselves. A common element in all of this is a psychopathic or selfish ego need.

Kidnapping, Hostage Situations, and Terrorism

You can be going about your business at work or in the office and become suddenly involved in some international or ideological kidnapping or hostage situation. The U.S. State Department reports hundreds of terrorist acts worldwide every year. If you're traveling outside the United States you should know about these potential trouble spots. Most of the time, sensitive areas and issues are featured in television and print news media. Within the United States, terrorist acts are most likely to be property crimes, not personal crimes. Political activists make their point through news coverage and public attention, not public outrage and intensive police pursuit. They achieve this goal by making news in events like the bombing of New York's World Trade Center. Killings are coincidental. They hope the public will react first with concern, then with an understanding and sympathy for their cause. This exerts political pressure in their favor. In most cases, public reaction is the opposite, such as the situation in Yugoslavia, Ireland, and the Middle East. The 1972 Munich Olympics hostage-taking of Israeli athletes failed to build support for the Arab cause and resulted in the deaths of both athletes and terrorists. Other examples include the murder of an invalid man on the *Achille Lauro* cruise ship; the midair bombing of 747 flight 103 over Lockerbe, Scotland, killing crew and passengers; hijacked TWA flight 847 and the beating death of an American sailor; and the bombing of the Marine barracks in Lebanon, killing hundreds of Marines.

Historically, though, terrorism has paid off enough to make it worthwhile and to motivate others to continue it. A few terrorists can exert enough pressure to destabilize a government. Fidel Castro began with a handful of followers and was able to take over Cuba for a generation. Victims are merely a means to the terrorist's political end. This is of little consolation to survivors who are not interested in and do not believe in their ideals.

Terrorists are usually a small number of close-knit fellow believers deeply committed to a common cause. They meet secretly and carefully plan sudden attacks to gain and hold media and public attention to influence and manipulate public opinion. Unfortunately, they are successful at least initially and at little cost to themselves or their sponsors. They use the element of surprise very well and know how best to manipulate news media to their advantage. In most cases they are few in number, and this simplifies communication and ensures secrecy. Sympathetic governments provide money and weapons, so they are well supplied. Terrorists disguise themselves as tourists, immigrants, or visiting scholars or executives. They dupe unknowing accomplices to carry parcels or luggage in which bombs are concealed.

In the United States most terrorist attacks have been by Puerto Rican separatists. Next is an assortment of fanatics supporting special interests such as "Earth First," "Up the IRS," "Earth Night Action," "Aryan Nation," and right-wing activists. According to FBI statistics, the most frequent terrorist targets are, in descending order: commercial establishments, military sites or personnel, federal buildings or property, educational institutions, places of entertainment, private residences, and security sites or staff. Types of attack include bombing, threats and hoaxes, hijacking, assassination, kidnapping, sniping, armed attack, barricades, and hostage taking. Tactics include breaking and entering, occupying buildings, theft of weapons and files, kidnapping and hostage taking, ambush attacks and assassination, street barricades, combat confrontation with police or the military, bombing, sabotage, and propaganda campaigns.

It is relatively rare for terrorists to take hostages in the United States, as happened in Iran in the late 1970s. It isn't practical when you are not in control of the immediate neighborhood. More common is hijacking and hostage taking by idealistic, angry, or delusional people. This gets immediate media attention. Most victims are tourists or workers who happened to be on the scene at the time. Risk of violence is proportionate to the stability and mental state of the assailants. The most violent incidents have involved jilted lovers or ex-husbands, fired employees, or evicted tenants. In a study of 82 officials victimized by terrorists, 31 were wounded, 18 killed, and 33 held hostage.

Hostage takers select one of four persons: *imposed status* (witnesses, judges, prosecutors, and investigators held "responsible"), *traditional* (public officials), *ideological* (recognized leaders in controversial movements), and *representative* (people who symbolize or are typical of a special or public interest).

How do you reduce your risk of becoming a terrorist hostage? Firms and agencies that may be targeted by terrorists should have their electronic and staff security systems tested regularly. There are steps you can take personally to reduce your risk of victimization:

1. Restrict your movements only directly to and from the workplace.

2. Control/limit exposure to the public and accessibility to terrorists.

3. Vary time of entry and exit and do not use the same entrance and exit daily.

If you are a prime target, these additional steps will further reduce risk:

4. Disinformation—misleading schedule information. When President Reagan was shot, his scheduled arrival by place and time was public information.

5. Deception. Use a different car but have the usual car or a look-alike appear to follow the schedule.

Bombs

It would be terrifying to be anywhere near an explosion like the World Trade Center in New York in 1993. There were 12,353 incidents involving explosives from 1985 to 1989. We know that not all bomb threats are reported, so there are probably many more incidents. The FBI reported 80,580 arson cases in one year. Some were fire bombings. A bomb is technically an *improvised explosive device* or IED. It can explode, burst into flame, or both. Electrical detonation is the most common trigger device, but sometimes a fast or slow-burning ignition fuse is used. Powerful plastic explosive is easily concealed in toys, cameras, radios, clothing, and luggage. Frequent places to conceal bombs are restrooms and lounges, lobbies, waiting rooms, mail rooms, and shipping and receiving departments. Likely containers include trash or garbage cans or dumpsters, potted plants, in or under desks, in file cabinets, or in packages.

Every workplace should have a bomb contingency plan. It can work the same way as a fire plan but should include securing the suspected bomb area, or if this is not known, a systematic search by local police after everyone is evacuated. *You should never go looking for a bomb yourself. You should never touch, handle, or move a suspected or real bomb.* Phone operators should be trained to remain calm when receiving a bomb threat and gather as much information as possible (location, type, time set, reason, etc.). Some provision to audiotape such calls can help identify the caller's voice. "Caller ID," a tracing service provided by some telephone companies, is a great help.

Riots

Being anywhere near a riot situation increases your risk of injury, even death. After the verdict of the first Rodney King trial was announced in Los Angeles, fifty-three people were killed in riots that followed. Many of the people injured and killed in the violence were not rioters themselves. The first rule to protect your own personal security is not being there. If you are in such a situation, get out of there as soon as possible. Do not panic. Maintain control of yourself and your vehicle if driving. If necessary, drive over curbs or off the street, but do so carefully. Do not drive into isolated areas or down streets unfamiliar to you. In most cases you will know of sensitive areas beforehand and if you must go in or near them you should study a map so you will know alternate routes. Keep your radio on. A police scanner is a plus.

Executive/Manager Security

Anyone in management, even of a convenience store, can be targeted as an example by terrorists to embarrass the firm and gain media attention. Executives have been kidnapped and held for ransom. Some have been assassinated to pay back the corporation for real or imagined wrongs. The terrorists have been misguided fanatics or disgruntled employees. Ironically, most managers and executives set themselves up, making themselves vulnerable to these incidents. They do so by behaving predictably—following the same daily routine makes it easy to be intercepted and taken hostage. Hostage takers can be very dangerous. Some Mid-East terrorists believe they are on a sacred mission and if they are killed in the act they go straight to heaven. Some hostage takers were employees, even security officers, who thought they could make a fortune and flee the country by kidnapping the boss.

How can managers be protected? As is true of all the risk situations in this book, *awareness* and *avoidance* are the major preventives. Danger areas are two: internal and external.

Internal Dangers

1. Unscreened, unknown employees, especially those who are new, have moved often, and have not held jobs long.

2. Disgruntled employees and former employees, especially loners who drink and have problems—and guns.

3. Smart insiders, especially those with access to scheduling information and office security.

External Dangers

1. Crowds in which perpetrators can hide, such as tours, public events, or committee meetings.

2. Deliveries to and pickups from the firm. A seemingly innocent delivery van blew up the World Trade Center in New York.

3. Service and repair specialists. Many a "bug" has been planted in executive offices by "innocent" repair men. The Boston Strangler gained entry into his victim's homes using this ploy.

Suggested Prevention Measures

1. *Anticipate.* Brainstorm how a manager or employee could be kidnapped or killed. List the possibilities. Consult with local police, who can probably add a few more. These are the target behaviors to prevent.

2. *Increased awareness by closer observation.* This includes *personal* (confidential scrutiny of employees most likely to react violently) and *electronic* (mechanical surveillance that is appropriate and least intrusive to employees, such as metal detectors, closed-circuit TV, etc.).

3. *Deter–Avoid.* Establish a security perimeter. As with medieval forts there should be rings or lines of defense from parking lot and street to entrance and inside rooms.

4. *Control–React.* There should be (a) a *response plan* for the target threats to a manager or employee, in ascending order from informal intervention within the firm to calling the police; (b) a *response team*, a pyramid-style activation plan branching out to involve more people as a threat situation develops and grows; and (c) *drills* to practice the plan on a quarterly basis.

● ● ●

Sexual Harassment

While sexual harassment has probably been around since cave men jeered at women walking by, it became a matter of public and political concern during the 1990s. Several incidents sparked this increased interest. There was the naïveté of an assortment of U.S. Senators during the Clarence Thomas–Anita Hill hearings, followed by the demeaning behavior of U.S. Navy officers at the Tailhook Association reception and reports of sexual abuse of women in the Persian Gulf campaign.

Sexual harassment is any unwanted sexual comment or gesture. The key word is *unwanted* and this depends solely on the victim's perception. In most cases victims are women, though anyone can be sexually harassed—men, children, and the elderly. Harassment is wrong for several reasons:

1. It is a form of discrimination, therefore illegal.

2. It is a misuse of management power, therefore unethical.

3. It is an indignity toward a fellow human being, therefore immoral.

4. It is a form of sustained stress, therefore physically and mentally harmful.

Why does it happen? Some mental health professionals see it as "soft rape" with the same basic motive: power. Some men harass women to test whether they are interested in them and in having sex with them. Too many men actually believe women like it. It can be a male bonding ritual such as in the Tailhook incident. It can be a pathetic, immature offer, a primitive threat, or a sadistic form of terrorism.

While sexual harassment is not a felony or crime that can be tried in criminal court, harassers can be held liable for damages in civil proceedings. The Equal Employment Opportunities Commission (EEOC) and the U.S. Supreme Court define two types of sexual harassment: *quid pro quo*, "this for that" or "something for something," whereby sex is used as barter to get or keep a job, promotion, or other benefits; and *hostile environment*, whereby work conditions are intimidating, stressful, or offensive specific to gender. Courts have held employers as liable as harassers, even when offenders are not employees but customers or visitors, if it can be shown they knew of or should have known of the harassment.

There is a three-pronged test to validate sexual harassment:

1. Harassment was sexual and a reasonable person would see it as sexual.

2. It was unwanted and unwelcome, not encouraged by the victim who informed the harasser of this fact.

3. The harassment continued anyway. It was not an isolated incident or single social blunder.

Sexual harassment on the street is a more difficult problem. Many times it is not witnessed, and legal definitions and enforcement are weak. It varies from a whistle, shout, or comment to unwanted physical touching. It goes beyond "nice dress" or "I like your hair that way" to vulgar sexual connotations that leave no doubt. Anyone who touches you in a way that a reasonable person would find sexual and unwanted can be charged with assault or battery. This goes beyond sexual harassment. Some suggestions:

1. When walking on the street, walk purposefully, upright, and businesslike. Look straight ahead, walk with normal pace, and in a straight line.

2. Avoid isolated high-risk areas such as side streets, park or garden paths with few people, construction sites, men's hangouts, or anywhere you've been harassed before. Cross the street before you pass any suspicious man or group of them, especially if they are loud or in a "fun" mood (remember Tailhook).

3. If you find yourself alone with a harasser with no escape, humanize and personalize yourself. Try this: "I'm a human being just like you. Why are you treating me like this?" This enables you to be articulate, exert some control—and it turns off many male chauvinists.

If he persists, shift into second with: "Look, I'm trying to reason with you. Do you want to get arrested?" If police intervene you will then have evidence that (a) you didn't welcome or encourage his advances, (b) you told him so in good faith, and (c) he continued anyway. Another strategy is to make a big scene. Public attention is a powerful weapon against harassers. If someone sexually touches you, scream. Make it the loudest, most shrill scream of your life. If a harasser jeers and glares at you, in a clear, cold, loud voice say: "Stop staring at me!"

4. Be friendly, but not inviting. A smile and greeting is okay, but don't linger on it, which to some strangers changes "welcome" to "I wanna."

5. This one's controversial: Many women feel they should be free to dress the way they want to, regardless of the effect it may have on some men. If you end up in court, the defense attorney can charge that you deliberately dressed provocatively. Even sunglasses to some males project a "loose, sexy" movie star or entertainer image.

Sexual harassment is learned behavior. It can therefore be unlearned. It is behavior deeply rooted in history and culture and reinforced with every generation. What is desperately needed is open, equal communication between men and women. Men have to be more attentive, sensitive listeners. Women have to be more articulate and clear. They must both meet each other halfway, a 50–50 blending of two equal, natural forces in dynamic balance.

CAMPUS CRIME

Violent and non-violent crimes described in this book occur in school settings, from playgrounds through high school and college. Children have been kidnapped from playgrounds, even from the classroom. Ted Bundy's last killings were in a college sorority house. Some offenses, such as date rape and sexual harassment, occur frequently on campus.

Date Rape

Dating is a normal social pastime, usually a pleasant shared experience based on mutual respect and trust. The trauma of date rape, unwanted sex, is made worse not only by the sexual assault, which is a crime, but also the indignity, humiliation, and violation of trust involved. Date rape is the major violent crime on college campus. If you are a student victimized by sexual assault on campus there are three sources of restitution:

1. Specific college or university policies and services
2. Police investigation, possible arrest, and prosecution
3. Civil suit for monetary damages

The school can hold a hearing and the accused can be disciplined or expelled if found guilty. This is independent of police investigation for criminal charges or civil suit by you for monetary damages. It is possible to pursue all three of these alternatives.

On-Campus Services

Most colleges and universities have specific policies and procedures for reporting, investigating, and processing sexual assault of students. Student health centers provide for immediate medical attention for injury and prevention of sexually transmitted diseases, directly or by referral to a nearby hospital. Most schools have therapists on campus to provide supportive psychotherapy. Some schools offer mediation services between victim and accused. The dean of students can arrange a change in housing if victim and accuser have rooms in the same building or nearby.

Police Investigation

Reporting a sexual assault to the police does not mean you must file charges, but the prosecuting attorney can charge a suspect and call you as witness. Delay in reporting a sexual assault can mean lost evidence (DNA specimen, color photo of bruises or injury, torn clothing, etc.). If you are assaulted off campus, you are in the jurisdiction of the local police and a 911 phone call will bring assistance. You may ask the police for a rape crisis counselor. Police investigation can lead to the criminal charge of rape or aggravated sexual battery.

Civil Suit

You can file a civil suit against your assailant for monetary damage based on pain and suffering. Consult an attorney to explore this alternative.

A nationwide survey of college students found that 42 percent had been "binge drinking"—consuming five or more drinks on one occasion—within two weeks of the study. About twice as many students in four-year colleges drank heavily as those in two-year or community colleges. Twice as many males were drinkers as females, and most were caucasian and fraternity members living on campus. Drinkers had significantly lower grade point averages than non-drinkers. About half of the survey sample reported memory lapse of drinking bouts and regretting behavior while drinking. One in four women reported engaging in sex they would have declined if not drinking. Sixteen percent stated alcohol contributed to being seduced. Reported marijuana use was 27 percent and cocaine 6 percent. The profile of a typical student sex offender: male caucasian fraternity member living on campus who binge drinks and is not going steady with one partner.

To minimize risk of sexual assault you should be aware of those contributing factors and avoid them. Other suggestions:

1. Know your date.

2. Establish and maintain clear, open communication from the beginning as to your likes and dislikes so you will not be misunderstood. You may want to be assertive (not offensive) and agree up front that there will be no sex.

3. If there is an unwanted sexual advance, make your disapproval known in a friendly but firm way.

4. If there is a sudden, unexpected sexual assault, react firmly, clearly and loudly saying you do *not* want to have sex. This should be crisp and matter-of-fact and not sound or seem like you're being coy or teasing.

5. If you are overpowered, say "No" loudly and repeatedly and push him away. Repeat your disapproval more pointedly (example: "Why are you doing this to me?"). You may feel frightened and helpless but you should voice and demonstrate your refusal, not only to deter your assailant but to prove later you did not consent and gave the assailant every opportunity to cease and desist.

6. Know important phone numbers, such as the campus police and local rape crisis line. Know where the campus

police are. They are open 24 hours on most campuses.

7. Don't let anyone talk you out of pressing charges if that's what you want to do.

8. Keep a coin in your wallet if public phones require one.

Colleges and universities have written policies that forbid sexual harassment and sexual misconduct. Harassment is unwanted, demeaning, or threatening verbal or physical gestures perceived as sexual by the victim. Sexual misconduct is any unwanted touching of a victim's breast, buttock, thigh, or genitalia, attempted or actual oral, anal, or vaginal penetration of a sexual nature by penis, finger, or object. The key word is *unwanted* and this means the act was by force, intimidation, or the victim's inability by mental or physical state to resist. Substance abuse (alcohol and/or drugs) by accuser, victim, or both does not excuse the crime. Sexual assault of a person "under the influence" *who does not consent* is a crime.

While you may feel shocked, violated, and justifiably outraged after a sexual assault, our legal system and school policies are based on fairness and due process. The accused must be given notice, reasonable time to prepare a defense, and the opportunity to present that defense at a fair hearing. Federal law requires both victim and accuser be informed of the decision. Both parties can appeal the decision. There can be concurrent proceedings, a hearing on campus and criminal court proceedings by police. Civil suit usually follows criminal proceedings so that founded charges can be used in civil court.

Most colleges and universities protect certain rights of both the victim and the accused:

1. To be informed of school policy, hearing procedure, consequences, and alternatives relative to sexual assault on

campus.

2. A fair and prompt hearing.

3. To know the names of all witnesses.

4. To have someone accompany him/her during the hearing.

5. A private, closed hearing and confidentiality of all proceedings.

6. To be informed of the decision.

- 7. To appeal the decision.

There are certain rights assured victims:

1. On request, a formal campus restraining order forbidding contact or harassment by the accused or his/her supporters.

2. To challenge the appointment and presence of any hearing officer who is a friend, fraternity brother or sorority sister, faculty advisor, or other person who may be biased for the accused.

3. To make a victim impact statement.

4. To be present for the entire duration of the hearing.

To establish due process most schools assure certain rights to the accused, such as:

1. To be presumed innocent until proven otherwise.

2. To remain silent.

3. To testify on his/her own behalf.

Sexually harassed students often report feeling abused or used, "dirty" and demeaned, victims of "mini-rapes." What can you do to prevent sexual harassment on campus? Check to ensure the school has a sexual harassment policy and procedures to deal with it. This policy should contain definitions, scope (faculty, staff, students), investigative procedures, and specified consequences. There should be regularly scheduled, documented orientation training and refresher sessions for all those covered by the policy. Where, to whom, and how violations are to be reported should be posted prominently on campus and readily available in brochures in traveled areas and the school's counseling center.

TOURISM AND TRAVEL

Most people look forward to a vacation. It is an opportunity to escape the stress of everyday life and enjoy a brief interlude away from it all. Planning it involves much wishful thinking and pleasant anticipation. This makes the trauma of crime more deeply painful. Just as crime doesn't discriminate among people—it can happen to anyone at any time—it also does not discrimate among places and can occur during life's otherwise most pleasurable times.

A sixteen-year-old Japanese student lost and looking for a Halloween party he had been invited to in a major city was shot and killed on the doorstep of a private home he approached—unarmed—to seek help. Tourists have been beaten, robbed, or killed when they became lost in rented cars from major airports. Children have been kidnapped from hotels, playgrounds, and theme parks. In 1991, 36,512 non-residents visiting Florida were victims of robbery, rape, murder, or other crimes. To be fair, Florida received forty million tourists every year, which means that about one of every thousand tourists was victimized.

Airports

More than a thousand airliners take off and land every day at most major airports. Airports are mini-cities where strangers come and go at a busy pace. Larger airports have their own jail where prisoners are held for local police or federal agents. The ingredients for an ideal crime scene are there: heavy traffic (vehicle and pedestrian), relative anonymity (better chance of escape), concentration of valuables (luggage, purses and wallets, airline tickets), distractions, and the hectic pace. Wherever there's a crowd and the chance of getting jostled, there is increased risk of pickpocketing and purse snatching. Some thieves work in teams, one to bump or distract you, the other to lift your valuables with a skilled velvet touch.

Here's a sampling of typical airport and other vacation crime risk situations:

1. *Rental cars* are an invitation to thieves when they have special license tags and stickers with the rental agency name. Tourists who lost their way have been robbed and killed. Ask the car rental clerk about areas to avoid. If he or she doesn't know, ask the airport security police. Mark danger areas on a map before you pick up the car and do not go anywhere near them. Study the map before you leave the airport.

2. *Parking lots* are high-risk areas, described in detail in Chapter 3. Park only in well-lighted areas nearest the parking lot attendant and notice where the nearest phone and public area are. If your rented car is in a dark or remote area, ask airport security to escort or watch you until you get in the car and drive away.

3. *At curb, counter, bar, restroom, and luggage claim area,* you may be distracted and easy prey for "snatch and run" attacks on your luggage, wallet, or purse. Beware of casual chats with friendly strangers at these vulnerable times. Smart crooks will use a confederate to involve you as they steal your belongings. Other distractions include staging an argument or fight with a confederate nearby, or spilling a

drink or ketchup on you. Another clever device is a "booster box," a large hollow suitcase open at the bottom and placed over your bag, which is then "boosted" away. You can see a thief leaving the scene and not know where your missing bag is! Mark bags with durable ID and distinctive colored ribbon. Put ID on the inside, too, to prove it's yours if a thief is caught in the act and has removed outside ID. Carry your wallet in a fanny pack worn in front.

4. *Sleeping* in any public place is another invitation to criminals, especially in darker low-traffic areas. Criminals can also sit unnoticed in waiting areas watching for the most promising target victims.

5. *Never agree to take anyone's package or bag into the terminal or on an airliner.* The friendliest person could be handing you illegal drugs, stolen goods—or a bomb. Incidentally, larger airports get one or two bomb threats every month. If ever near a package thought to contain a bomb, *do not touch it.* Get out of the way. The local bomb squad has padded uniforms, armor plated disposal bins, and trained dogs that sniff for explosives.

6. *Don't carry weapons into airports.* Metal detectors are a necessary annoyance to detect bombs and weapons. Many guns detected are in non-criminal women's handbags. Carrying weapons in an airport is a serious federal offense despite any permit from a local court. Chemical sprays are also forbidden because of the possibility of accidental discharge in the enclosed cabin of a plane. Even police officers authorized to carry weapons must identify themselves and inform the airline of weapons they carry.

Restrooms

Having luggage, a wallet, or a purse in easy reach while you "answer nature's call" is an ideal setup for the "snatch and run." If you are the only person in the restroom, an outside lookout can secure the door while the thief robs you.

Lodging and Leisure Activities

You should use the same security precautions in hotels, motels, cruise ships, trains, buses, resorts, museums, theaters, and restaurants as for airports. You are vulnerable to theft at registration and checkout desks, ticket lines, and in restaurants. Crooks will look and dress like tourists, or use special disguises. The friendly fellow pointing out your location on the map you are holding can have his other hand in your bag or pocket. Hotel thieves often wear business suits and carry attaché cases. If alone in your room and hotel staff knock at the door, ask for name and purpose and tell them to wait while you call the front desk to confirm. A crook won't wait, but hotel staff will, even if a bit annoyed with you. There are portable motion detector alarms you can install on the door of your room to prevent intrusion by anyone who might have a key or is able to open the door. Children have been kidnapped walking down hotel hallways, grabbed and dragged into a room. Always have your children walk in front of you so you can see them and anyone who approaches them. Unpopulated or less traveled back areas are always danger areas. These are violent criminals' territories where they feel safe from interruption.

Shops, Gas Stations, and Convenience Stores

In addition to security procedures described in this chapter, there are special risks while shopping and stopping at gas stations and convenience stores. If both arms are full of packages, a thief can more easily rob you of your purse or wallet. If you are wearing a dress, clever thieves will knock you down in such a way your dress will fly up. Most women will by learned reflex first pull the dress down, giving the thief a few more seconds to rob them and run away. As described in Chapter 3, your car can be quickly stolen if you leave keys in the ignition while you go to pay for gas or buy convenience items.

Boating

Boats are stolen right off the dock, and parts can be taken from them at the pier or on land while boats are being painted or overhauled. Drug runners like to use a variety of boats. They have been known to hijack boats at sea and, in extreme cases, kill boat owners and guests. Drugs are a multi-*billion*-dollar business worth the risk to drug kingpins. Preventive practices include:

1. Have a radio transceiver and master its use.
2. Keep tuned to the Coast Guard frequency.
3. Get a cellular phone for emergency use and know the nearest Coast Guard station's land line phone number.
3. Remain alert to your surroundings.
4. Consider carrying weapons if you will be at sea overnight or in international waters.
5. If approached by a vessel that is in any way suspicious, phone the nearest Coast Guard station, give your position, explain the situation, and tell them you'll call back when it is resolved.

Hiking and Camping

Hiking and camping are for many an escape from busy everyday living, from phones and noise. If in bear country, there are precautions to take, such as making noise and wearing a bell around your neck. Knowing "bear facts" also helps. Never get between a mother bear and a cub. A few people are killed by bears every year, but many more die at the hands of other humans. Backpackers have been robbed or killed by "friendly" strangers along the trail. Remote locations make it more difficult to report crime and apprehend suspects. A CB radio or cellular phone provides a useful communications link in case of injury or wrongdoing. Check in on a regular schedule with a forest ranger or local police, giving your position each time. You should also have the number of the nearest Fish and Wildlife Officer. You should make contact with these support services days before your trip.

Drug Harvests, Poachers, and You

If you travel off the beaten path you should be aware of two multi-million-dollar illegal industries you could happen upon that could cost you your life. You might wander onto a drug crop at harvest time. The area is likely to be well guarded by people with sophisticated weapons. Remote areas are favored for growing these illegal crops. *Poaching* is illegally taking animals or birds out of season or which are protected species. If you're lucky the poachers will be a small group of locals who play dumb and hope you don't notice what they're doing is illegal. You'll be in up to your neck if you happen upon organized crime in a high-profit business. Organized poachers use helicopters or aircraft, four-wheel-drive vehicles or snowmobiles, automatic weapons, and sophisticated night vision optics. It's like finding yourself on a James Bond movie set. But this one will be real, and you'll be there, where you shouldn't be.

What's the probability you could have anything to do with poachers? A dozen were apprehended in Alaska trying to trade drugs for walrus tusks. Most frequent products are illegal meat (venison, elk, moose, or antelope out of season), "caviar" from Mississippi River paddlefish roe (worth $600 a pound in Europe), bear bones and claws for jewelry, elk antlers for furniture, mounted big game animal heads and eagle feather headdresses, live falcons (one fetched $100,000 in the Middle East), and black or grizzly bear gall bladders ($40 a gram in Asia).

What can you do if you come upon poachers in a remote area? If you have a CB or cellular phone, it would be wise to phone in and check them out before they see you. Chances are they'd be making some noise and sound carries well in the wilderness. This is another reason for you to exert care and caution wherever you are. In the bush, additional awareness is needed for sights, sounds, and smells, a good preventive practice to protect against minimally harmful animals and predatory humans.

Vacation Scams

There are clever crooks who are constantly devising schemes to part you from your money or property. Here is a sampling:

Key switch is a clever scam whereby a friendly person helps you load your luggage into a coin locker at an airport, bus, or train station. Some even have the exact change or put your coins into the locker's coin slot for you. What could be wrong with such kindness? The key you are handed is to an empty locker. The crook palms your key. When you are a safe distance away, your luggage is a sitting duck.

A *private guide* offers to take you wherever you want to go and at a reasonable price. Some of these people are honest, others are thieves who rob you and leave you lost on an unknown road in a strange land. It may cost a few bucks more to use licensed tour guides and known firms, but it's usually far safer.

Phony travel services. Beware of travel agencies who use direct mail and sometimes television commercials to promote "too good to be true" vacation offers. Some try for your credit card number, others for cash, or both. Sophisticated con artists use 800 numbers or a post office box, which are easy to cancel and hard to trace. By the time enough consumers complain, crooks are on the road to the next location. If you think you may be the victim of a vacation scam, report it to your local postal inspector if the crime was done by mail, the phone company if by phone, and local police if through a newspaper ad.

LET THERE BE LIGHT!

There is a simple security rule for home, work, and play: light discourages crime and darkness encourages it. Are your home and workplace well-lighted? There should be good outside lighting where you park and walk and around buildings to expose anyone lurking there. Trees and bushes should be trimmed low to provide a clear field of view. Inside lighting should illuminate hallways and stairwells, and these should be free of obstructions and hiding places. Why not form a committee and do a security survey with a local police officer?

CPTED is *crime prevention through environment design,* special designs for grounds, building structure, floor and office plans for maximum security. These designs have no adverse effect on business, are as appealing to consumers as non-security design, and better protect both the public and employees. Major features are good lighting, clear visibility, low natural barriers, and color-coded wide aisles.

• • •

USEFUL RESOURCES

Clede, W. (1993). "Modern Poaching Is Big Time Crime." *Law and Order,* May 1993, pp. 98–99.

MacHovec, F. J. (1992). *Security Services, Security Science.* Springfield, IL: Charles C. Thomas.

Seuter, E. J. (1992). "Taking the Bang out of Bomb Threats." *Security Management,* March 1992, pp. 47–51.

CHAPTER 5

Afterwards

Using the information and suggestions in the preceding chapters will help you avoid crime situations and cope with them if you are ever a crime victim. They dealt with the *before* and *during* phases of a crime. This chapter will help you with the aftermath, the short- and long-term effects of crime victimization.

REPORT EVERY CRIME

Every crime should be reported. Every criminal should be prosecuted. There is no other way to stop crime. There are more than ten million arrests every year, 500,000 for violent crimes and two million for property crimes. It is estimated that less than half of all crimes committed are actually reported. That's a sad statistic. Even more sadly, it hasn't changed much for decades. Victims report half the violent and household crimes and only three of ten personal crimes. It may be that victims are so relieved they weren't hurt or killed or the losses greater they just write it off as a bad experience. This does not help the next victim, who may be hurt or killed.

Unreported crime means another criminal is loose on the street. Prompt reporting means police can quickly patrol the area and alert officers elsewhere to look for and detain suspects. It improves security for everyone and builds a useful database for local, state, and federal agencies and legislators to see trends and take timely action to control and prevent crime.

Women report violent crime more than men, at a 60–40 ratio. Reporting rates of caucasians, African-Americans, Hispanics, and Asian-Americans are about the same. Youths between 12 and 20 report only 15 percent of thefts. Men and women between 50 and 64 years old report more crime than any other age group. The reporting rate by age per 1,000 victims: 38 for ages 12–19, 50 for ages 20–34, 56 for ages 35–49, 64 for ages 50–64, and 59 for age 65 and older.

Victims who report violent crime give these reasons for doing so: to stop the incident, to recover their property, and to prevent further crime against them. Reasons for not reporting violent crime: the offender didn't succeed, the victim considers the crime too personal or private, fear of reprisal, police seen as ineffective ("What's the use?"), and reporting seen as inconvenient and time-consuming.

If you are ever raped, get help immediately afterward from the local rape crisis center (do you have the number right now?), call the police (911), or go to the emergency room of the nearest hospital. *Go as you are*. Do *not* wash or wipe *anything*. Every rapist should be arrested, convicted, and locked up, right? If you remove or change clothing, shower, wash, or wipe off anything you destroy important evidence, like DNA in body fluids (semen, blood) that can identify the criminal and guarantee conviction. You may think you look like an animal or even feel like one, but the beast who committed the crime deserves to be hunted down.

POLICE INVESTIGATION AND REPORTS

While almost always inconvenient and sometimes disturbing, no criminal can be pursued and caught unless the police know who to look for. It is absolutely necessary to provide them with a detailed account of the crime. Without this, it is almost impossible to apprehend suspects, especially as soon after the crime as possible. Police interview methods have improved greatly, and in most cases a female officer will talk to women who have been raped and notify the local rape crisis center. In many cases a therapist or volunteer (often a rape victim herself) can be with you as you are interviewed and afterward to explain the legal process to you and help start you on the road to recovery. Medical and psychiatric services will also be available for treatment of injuries and medication should you need or want them.

The police interview is a way of recreating the crime, ensuring all the evidence is taken at the crime scene, describing injuries to the victim, and identifying the assailant. For these reasons, it is necessary that you go into minute detail, mentioning anything and everything that you remember. What you may think is trivial can be an important clue and lead to incriminating evidence. To remember clearly and vividly is to relive the crime, and that's bound to be unpleasant. Reporting it to a stranger can be embarrassing and humiliating. Most police interviewers are sensitive to this and also to the likelihood you will be upset. While it is a first for you, the interviewing officer has been through the process many times and has had extensive training to gather as much information in the least time. Some of the questions may seem pointed or personal. Though unpleasant or even painful, it is the cost to you to apprehend and stop criminals from victimizing others. It is your duty as a citizen and as a fellow human being to others who may be victimized in the future.

THE NEWS MEDIA

If a crime is especially newsworthy there will be newspaper and TV reporters with notepads and cameras. Most news desks monitor police radio frequencies and reporters can be on the scene within minutes of the crime. Remember when UN troops landed in the middle of the night in Somalia and were greeted with reporters, cameras, and floodlights? You could be similarly featured if the crime is considered to be of high audience interest. If this happens and it makes you uncomfortable, ask the police to inform the media you do not want to be photographed or interviewed. If you tell them yourself, you could still be on television news, videotaped as you tell them.

Afterwards, news media may phone you or, worse still, be at your door asking for an interview. If you don't want to be interviewed, tell them so firmly but calmly. Better still, have someone else "run interference" and tell them for you. If you say anything at all to them you might still be quoted, or by clever manipulation answers may be extracted from you without you having time to think them through. Only a few seconds can be used from a half-hour interview; quotes might be used out of context and differ in meaning from what you really think and feel. You may consent to being interviewed. That and the police interview can be the start of your recovery from the trauma of the event. And media coverage of the crime can help apprehend a criminal still at large and alert others to their own personal danger. It may stimulate someone's morbid curiosity and add to the glut of crime subject matter already in print and visual media. But the important difference is that your story is in the public interest, in the real world, and part of crime prevention and control. That separates it from the excess of media violence and sexuality. Here are guidelines for dealing with the media:

1. *Know what you want to say and what you do not want to say.* Take time to gather your wits, to center yourself. Don't let them rush you. Pauses and what reporters consider unimportant information will be edited out anyway. If you feel yourself getting upset, *say so.* It helps you vent the feeling and regain composure. If it gets overwhelming, say so and terminate the interview. You've already been through too much, and no one has the right to violate your dignity for their own ratings.

2. *Keep it simple.* Using clear, simple language minimizes misunderstanding and makes it more likely you will be quoted accurately.

3. *Be brief.* Don't make a speech. Very little of what you say will be used anyway. This also means you won't be "on the spot" long.

4. *Expect to be manipulated verbally* toward more sensational statements or gory details. News in newspapers and on television is a big business. The raw material, the stuff it's made of, is "hot copy" because that's what sells. Don't hesitate to say "I don't know" or to correct interviewers with a relaxed (not sarcastic or antagonistic) "I didn't say that" or "that's not what I mean" or "that's not what happened." Be prepared to terminate the interview when you're ready, tired, upset, or are repeating yourself. Respectfully resist the request "But I have only a few more questions." Beware of "one final question"—it can be the most provocative. Try saying, "I'm sorry, I'm too upset to continue." Be friendly but firm. It's your life and you have a right to privacy.

5. *Play it straight.* Don't try to manipulate, slant,

exaggerate, lie, or be clever. Be yourself; be honest. Putting a "spin" on anything can destroy your credibility.

6. *Rehearse* any prepared statement if you have time to do so. Get feedback from a trusted friend or loved one so you sound and look the way you want. You could have your attorney, spouse, family member, or friend make the statement for you or be at your side when you do.

7. *Stay cool.* Try to be emotionally insulated from probing questions and comments that might upset you or prevent you from completing your statement to your satisfaction or imparting the information you feel is important.

8. *Attend to your appearance.* If on TV, some makeup (even for men) prevents a shiny face and baggy or sunken eyes. Without it you could look like a corpse. Don't wear sparkly jewelry, large areas of white or closely striped clothing. They "flash" on screen. Ground yourself solidly in a chair or stand upright, feet slightly apart, balanced. A secure posture will help you feel secure. Look at the interviewer. Avoiding eye contact suggests to viewers you may be lying or feel guilty because you directly or indirectly provoked the crime.

COURT

Becoming Court Smart

Being *court smart* is an important part of being *street smart.* Many victims feel traumatized twice—once by the crime itself and again by the legal process, from police interview to the trial. Police, lawyers, and judges are aware of the added stress involved, but court proceedings are the most civilized way the whole world has found to be fair and just to victims and defendants. If you understand the legal process it can work for you and become part of your recovery. Being court smart will minimize and hopefully eliminate the stress of court proceedings. It may help to have a victim advocate with you before, during, and after your testimony. Meet with the prosecuting attorney. He or she will go over information needed in your testimony and the questions that need to be asked. You will then know what to expect in court. You may find it helpful to attend some other trial held in the same room in which you will testify. Doing these things will reduce your anxiety and help prepare you for your own day in court.

There are three kinds of courts in which you may be asked or expected to testify:

1. *Criminal courts* try cases of *felonies*, the most serious crimes punishable by death or imprisonment for a year or more, and *misdemeanors*, less serious offenses punishable by fine or incarceration in local jails usually for less than a year.

2. *Civil courts* hear cases to settle disputes and ensure restitution of loss, damage, or injury. Victims can sue a convicted felon in civil court for damages resulting from the crime.

3. *Juvenile and/or Family Court.* Juvenile offenders, because of their age, are not tried in criminal court but have adjudication hearings in these less formal courts.

Civil and criminal court proceedings are based on the *adversarial system*, a centuries-old Greco-Roman tradition, whereby defense and prosecution argue before a judge or jury. Only the judge, or jury if it is a jury trial, is the "trier of fact" who decides the case. A *bench trial* is when a judge alone reaches a verdict (decision) of guilt or innocence. Defendants can request either a bench or jury trial.

Because the central focus of this book is crime, what follows describes criminal court proceedings. Court is a world that differs from ours. It uses a different language and different rules. You will be a stranger there, and the state or prosecuting attorney will be your guide. He or she represents the state against the defendant, who will be represented by the attorney for the defense. Your role in the courtroom drama is to describe what happened before, during, and after the crime. That, with evidence from the crime scene and any witness testimony, is the basis for the state's charges against the suspect.

But this drama is staged according to strict rules enforced by the judge. It begins long before the trial with the arrest of the defendant who is interrogated by police after being read his or her rights, called Miranda rights. Usually within a day or two the defendant appears before a magistrate for a preliminary arraignment or initial court appearance. There, charges are formally announced and the defendant is informed of the right to counsel and to a preliminary hearing, usually within the next ten days. Bail is set at this time and defendants who can make bail are released from custody. One way to prevent suspects from disappearing into the sunset is to raise the amount of bail beyond their ability to pay. That way they remain in jail until trial. Those who skip town to escape prosecution are said to have "jumped bail" and arrest warrants are issued for them. Preventive detention is sometimes used to keep defendants in jail if the court feels they are likely to commit crimes if free on bail during the pretrial period.

At the preliminary hearing a magistrate presides and the prosecutor must prove there is probable cause, reasonable grounds to believe the suspect committed the crime. It is at this time evidence must be presented to substantiate the charges. This is when you will be asked to testify, with any witnesses and physical or "hard" evidence. During this hearing the defense does nothing but listen and learn what to expect later in court. Preliminary hearings are not a guaranteed due process; they aren't held in all court systems. Even where it is standard procedure defendants can choose to waive their right to one and either plead guilty or plea bargain, stopping the trial process altogether.

Learning each other's strengths and weaknesses is called *the discovery process.* The defense attorney can cross-examine you at the preliminary hearing to challenge and void probable cause and block further action (the trial) but rarely does so. It is usually difficult to keep a case from proceeding to trial, but the case can stop here if there is insufficient grounds to proceed or if you, the victim, or key witnesses do not want to continue. If probable cause is established the magistrate *binds over* the case to *felony* or *trial court.* Even then the process can be stopped if the defense sees the defendant is likely to be found guilty or the prosecution sees its case as too weak to get a conviction. Then both sides plea bargain a sentencing agreement for a guilty plea, usually for a less serious charge and less prison time. If both sides agree to this out-of-court conviction, there is no need to go to trial.

Let's assume the case is scheduled to go to trial. This is the most formal of court proceedings. The defense may ask for a change of venue to move the trial to another jurisdiction if it is felt the court or jury is biased where the alleged crime was committed. At trial, defendants plead guilty, not guilty, or *nolo contendere,* and they are represented by counsel, free of charge if they cannot afford it. Ted Bundy represented himself and impressed the judge, but was eventually executed—an expensive ego trip. It's a standard joke among lawyers that "anyone who represents himself has a fool for a client."

A guilty plea is carefully checked by the judge to ensure it is voluntary, intelligent, and informed. A not guilty plea allows the defense attorney to make pretrial motions to the judge requesting evidence obtained illegally be disallowed. Standing silently and saying nothing when asked by a judge how you plead is considered not guilty. *Nolo contendere* ("no contest") is equivalent to a guilty plea but eliminates the defendant being sued later in civil court by victims. *Nolle* or *nol pros* is a prosecutor's decision, approved by the court, not to prosecute a case. *Overcharging* is charging many crimes committed at the same time, not all of which can be proven.

Court is always a verbal battle between two forces, the defense and the prosecution (or, in civil court, the plaintiff). It is a simple, direct confrontation between two adversaries who do their utmost to prove the defendant is guilty or not guilty, to be convicted or acquitted. The ground rules are established court procedures, requirements of specific laws, and the rules of evidence. There is no middle ground, and you are on one side of that verbal battleground. Our system of justice is based on the premise that suspects are innocent until proven guilty in a court of law. What you may not know is the test of proof in criminal cases is *beyond a reasonable doubt,* and that means more than 90 percent certainty, the highest test. The test in civil cases is *clear and convincing* (75% certain) or *preponderance of evidence* (more than 50% certain).

Attorneys speak in turn to present their cases, subject to correction by the judge if either departs from proper procedure. First there are *opening statements,* a summary by both sides of what they hope to prove. Next is *direct examination,* the initial interrogation of victim and witnesses by the prosecuting attorney and any witnesses for the defense. The opposing attorney can go over a victim's or witness's direct testimony by *cross examination.* If it's a contested case there can be verbal ping-pong back and forth over evidence and testimony in *redirect examination.* That can be challenged or questioned by the opposing attorney in *recross examination.* This can lead to *rebuttal* and its counterpoint *surrebuttal.*

Verbal fireworks in this courtroom battle are about evidence for and against the defendant, its "admissibility," "abundance," and the "weight" it should be given. What is evidence? It includes statements, facts, and objects such as weapons, stolen property, fingerprints, and victim and witness testimony that prove or disprove a crime occurred and the guilt of the person who committed that crime. To be *admissible* it must be *relevant*, proving a fact; *credible* or *competent*, being valid (true of and by itself) and reliable (true in this and other cases); and *material*, directly related to the case. *Circumstantial evidence* is indirect and inferential, pointing toward a fact but not enough to firmly establish it. *Direct* or *hard evidence* is definite and irrefutable of and by itself such as finger, foot, or tire prints, blood or semen samples, stolen goods, photos or videotapes, and consistent victim and witness reports.

In the last phase of a jury trial, before jurors leave to be *sequestered* (meet in private) to *deliberate* (discuss, then decide) on a verdict, the judge will *charge* or *instruct* them. The principles of law involved that should be considered in reaching a verdict in the case are explained. A *hung jury* is one unable to reach a verdict. *Acquittal* is a court decision of a not guilty verdict. An *anonymous jury* is specially called in sensitive cases where identity and personal information of jury members is not made available to the defendant. A *grand jury* is a group of sixteen to twenty-three citizens who meet at the call of a prosecutor to decide probable cause to indict on criminal charges (whether a crime has been committed).

Defendants found guilty are usually *sentenced* a month or two after the trial. There are two choices: prison or probation. If prison, the judge has several choices: *determinate, fixed*, or *flat sentence*, for a specified number of years; *indeterminate*, for a range of time such as two to five years; *concurrent*, merging separate prison terms together such as a two-year and two five-year sentences into one five-year term; *consecutive*, adding separate prison terms such as a two-year and two five-year sentences for a twelve-year sentence. *Habitual offender laws* apply to persons with several prior convictions and provide for additional prison terms. In most cases, one fourth to one third of a served sentence can be dropped for good behavior. *Restitution* is financial payment to victims or community work prescribed by the court. *Retribution* is punishment fitting the crime, sometimes called *just deserts*.

Conditions of parole/probation are the rules to be followed while on parole (excarceration, after incarceration) or probation (instead of incarceration). Violating these rules is in itself a violation of law and may result in charges, trial, and imprisonment if convicted. The *parole/probation officer,* or PO, is a corrections specialist who makes presentence reports and supervises and counsels those on parole or probation in the community. Crime victims find it helpful to maintain contact with their assailant's PO to learn of parole hearings, where victim testimony is welcomed.

Can you imagine situations where you yourself may have to commit a crime to save a life or to prevent a greater crime? Such cases involve a *necessity defense*, when committing a crime is the "lesser of two evils." It originated in life or death survival situations when someone was sacrificed to save the lives of others. There are two classic cases: a ship's crew in 1842 threw fourteen passengers overboard to prevent sinking a lifeboat; and in 1844 three starving shipwrecked men killed and ate a seventeen-year-old cabin boy. There is also a *duress defense*, when you are forced to commit a crime without your consent, such as Patty Hearst, a hostage who participated in a bank robbery armed and dressed like the gang or cult that held her captive.

There are several movies with graphic courtroom conflict that can help you understand the world of law and court procedures: *The Verdict* (1982) with Paul Newman and James Mason; *Witness for the Prosecution*, the 1957 version with

Charles Laughton, Tyrone Power, and Marlene Dietrich or the 1982 version with Ralph Richardson, Deborah Kerr, Beau Bridges, and Diana Rigg; *Jagged Edge* (1985) with Glenn Close and Jeff Bridges. Check your local videotape rental store; they're worth seeing and you can playback and review in-court sections. *Verdict* is about a medical malpractice case in an American court. *Witness for the Prosecution* is a murder case in a British court, and *Jagged Edge* has a similar plot but an American setting.

Let's move from criminal to civil court proceedings. Courts determine responsibility for injury, physical or economic. *Negligence* is a frequent theme and proving it requires that the defendant could or should have known there was risk and did nothing to correct it. Crime victims can sue in civil court for medical bills and periods of unemployment because of injuries from the crime. *Compensatory damages* are financial judgments against a defendant because of negligence or wrongdoing. *Punitive damages* are specified by a civil court as punishment for wrongful acts.

Coping in Court

All the tips described earlier to help you cope with news media also apply to courtroom procedure. A major difference is that you do not have the freedom to decline to answer questions. The trial process is intentionally adversarial, two sides each trying for a single victory. In criminal court, as a victim, you will be questioned and cross-examined by the defense attorney who represents the alleged criminal. Those questions can be direct or indirect, pointed or subtle, hypothetical and off the wall, misleading, or with truth and errors intertwined. It's open season because you are in an adversarial situation in that strange world of law. Most lawyers advise victims and witnesses to keep answers short and simple and not to over-answer or volunteer additional information. Doing so can lead off on tangents and muddy the proceedings.

The prosecuting attorney (your side) will inform you beforehand of information needed and the questions likely to be asked by both sides. It's a good idea to rehearse them with the prosecutor before trial. *Always remember* that attorneys are trained to champion their side and some (not all) do so forcefully. Don't take it personally. They don't hate you. They're just trying to win, although maybe too hard. If you get upset on the stand don't hesitate turning to the judge and saying so or asking for a moment to regain control. Asking for a glass of water not only is acceptable in court but also gives you a few moments to regain composure.

If there is a microphone on the witness stand, *use it.* Do not slouch in the witness chair. It suggests you don't care or you're a slob. Don't lean forward and down. It can give the judge or jury the impression that you feel guilty or are responsible for the crime. Don't press your lips to the microphone like a rock star. It muffles your voice, making you sound confused and uncertain. It shouldn't be more than a foot from your mouth. Speak slower than your usual conversational speed. Your voice is being transmitted through the sound system. Words spoken too quickly run into each other, sounding muddled and difficult to understand.

Look at the attorney when questions are asked, but when you answer look at the judge or jury if it's a jury trial. Some attorneys stand between you and the jury to obstruct their view of you, or will walk there hoping you will look at them and not at the jury. In rare cases an opposing lawyer who can't overcome your testimony may probe for weaknesses in your character or even focus on your courtroom behavior: "I notice you hesitated before answering that last question. Is that because you are not sure of the facts?"

There are many factors and forces in any court case that you may not understand. The verdict may not please you. Criminals plea bargain to lesser charges and the weight of evidence may not be sufficient for a maximum sentence. Prisons are overcrowded and there is increasing use of "diversion" into community work, group homes, and supervised probation. A study of thirty-five court systems showed considerable variation in sentencing for the same crime. Convictions occurred in 70 to 80 percent of cases. The time from arrest to final disposition varied from four to fifteen months.

YOU IN CRISIS

Being involved in a crime as a victim or witness can be a stressful personal crisis, especially if the crime was a sudden, violent situation. Police and security experts refer to these as *critical incidents*, severe stress situations that overwhelm normal coping mechanisms and emotional controls. They've been described as awake nightmares, deeply disturbing experiences with marked negative psychological effects. Impact is increased when the incident is unexpected and there is extreme violence.

Being street smart is anticipating what might happen and deciding in advance or as quickly as you can what you choose to do. It is easier and quicker to react in crisis if you've gone over similar situations in your head beforehand and mentally rehearsed what you would want to do and not do. Even then it isn't so simple or easy because most crimes happen so suddenly. Consider two of the most feared situations, rape and aggravated assault. Assume you have no weapons, there's no escape, and no one is there to help you. These are big "ifs" and in real life you'll probably have more options. But it's most helpful to imagine the worst case scenario and prepare for it. Then whatever happens will be less stressful.

In the rape situation, pinned and helpless, you could vomit, defecate, or urinate. You could fake submitting, and if one hand is free, grab his scrotum and squeeze with all your might. A woman in Detroit, confronted in the middle of the night by a rapist, put a tight vise grip on it and would not let go. The rapist fell several times on his way to the door with her firmly attached to him. It is excruciatingly painful and disabling, more than you may have realized. Athletes struck there have fainted from the extreme pain. An Alaskan Eskimo told of how a fox can kill a wolf: Cornered, with no escape, the fox waited for the wolf to attack, mouth wide. At that precise moment the fox closed its needle-like teeth on the wolf's tongue. The fox clamped its jaws tightly shut. The wolf swung its head back and forth and in doing so tore out its tongue. Gruesome? Yes. But the innocent fox lived and the predatory wolf died. It is a fitting parable.

With respect to crime and your victimization, as we've discussed throughout this book, all things are relative. You should not—and have no right to—shoot an unarmed thief, because your life is not in danger. When it is there is an array of possibilities for you to consider. More alternatives to choose from mean more self-confidence and greater security. Naked in bed with a stronger person overpowering you, you still have your hands and the will to live. A thumb probed deep into an eye socket is also extremely painful. These tactics may be disgusting to you, but the alternatives are worse.

If struck hard in the aggravated assault, *go down*. Sit down or fall down. If the motive is theft, you must decide whether to give up your property or risk injury or death by resisting. Managing your own fall gives you partial or complete control of the fall. If someone knocks you down you are more likely to hit your head or break bones. In both the rape and assault situations you could also yell and scream, loud and shrill. This increases the risk of the assailant hitting you harder to shut you up. It's a judgment call that depends on the circumstances at the moment. Every crime situation is different, just as your response in each will differ with time, place, your position, weapons, and the severity of the threat to your life.

All of this is to prepare you for the question: What is your usual reaction to sudden, extreme stress? Your stress reaction is unique to you. In crisis you will need to minimize or control it. Reactions vary from getting shaky and tearful, the heart pounding, breathing rapidly, going blank paralyzed with fear, or striking out in rage and being unable to stop. Defending yourself requires that you know your typical physical and psychological reactions to sudden stress.

Next, it is helpful to know about steps in personality development everyone goes through that can be affected by a personal crisis. The psychologist Abraham Maslow formulated need levels of normal personality development from infancy to adulthood. There are five:

1. *Survival,* the need for food, air, warmth, and shelter, to be dry and held comfortingly close, and satisfied with the tender, loving care given most babies.

2. *Safety and security,* the need to be physically safe from danger, satisfied in early childhood by a sheltered home free from noise and accidents, "nesting" behavior.

3. *Emotional support,* the "apron strings" phase when children are most comfortable in the presence of others, satisfied by sitting close, a reassuring physical touch, or holding a hand.

4. *Self-esteem,* the need to belong, to be accepted, approved, and recognized. It is "family feeling" satisfied by a stable family system and membership in groups—church or temple, service or fraternal groups, clubs or gangs.

5. *Self-actualization,* the need to have a unique self-identity—the best you—and realize your full potential as that

person.

Think of these five needs as a stairway of five steps. You progress upward through these steps from infancy to adulthood. In a crisis situation, as impact increases, you are likely to tumble down the stairs. The first thing to go is self-actualization because you are powerfully and suddenly victimized, no longer in control of yourself or the situation. Next is identification with your group, as rape victims who feel dehumanized, treated impersonally, and more like animals than humans. Fear and terror with no one to protect you pushes you back through level 3. As violence increases, you are down to levels 2 and 1 where survival is the remaining need and you must fight or die. You can see this destructive force in television news coverage in the faces and behaviors of victims of war, fires, riots, and accidents, as well as violent crime. If you or someone you know are victimized, knowing Maslow's need levels can help restore normal functioning. Watch for signs of need and take steps to satisfy them.

RECOVERY

Whether you are the victim of a violent crime and physically injured, or suffer a loss by theft or vandalism without personal attack, there will be psychological after-effects. Family, friends, and others who care will support you and help put the unpleasant experience behind you. In most cases, psychological effects slowly fade over time. If the crime was severe you should have regular sessions with a licensed mental health professional. It's more efficient and more effective to get help from a trained professional, and it will speed your recovery. It may help you to view your victimization as bad luck, the unfortunate consequence of being a good person in a bad situation beyond your control. Life is full of such situations, good and bad. *Trauma* is the clinical term for something unexpected that is bad. Crime can be a matter of fate, a misfortune for which you are not to blame.

Poets and philosophers have described life as a wheel of fortune. Carl Orff set medieval monks' poems to music in *Carmina Burana*, music you may want to hear. It begins with "O Fortuna," a musical image of life as a great rotating wheel of good and bad luck. Reflecting on life's good fortune and misfortune, Edgar Guest wrote: "I don't like the cards dealt me, but I like the game and I want to play." Whatever happens to you, you must pick up the pieces and move on. That is more easily said than done, but it is nevertheless true. Life *does* go on. It *is* worth living. Painful memories *do* fade.

Psychological Effects

Let's take a closer look at what can happen to you psychologically as a crime victim:

1. *Feeling violated.* Even if your car has been stolen or your home broken into while you were away, most victims feel "penetrated" or "violated." Drawers in disarray, your clothing disturbed, closets left open—all are a direct invasion of your privacy and your mind and person. Those injured in a personal attack often feel like an animal attacked by a predator.

2. *Loss, grief.* A car or prized possession suddenly missing causes negative effects in thinking (loss) and feeling (grief). Favorite things are like old friends and they can be deeply missed. Even when recovered, there can be a feeling they—and therefore *you*—have been violated. Your stolen car returned dented and spattered, with empty beer cans and fragments of fast food on the seats and floor, may bring tears to your eyes, and when you drive it, it isn't the same

anymore. It is as if the car has died.

3. *Dissociation.* This is an automatic (involuntary) psychological defense many crime victims experience, and it can take several different forms. *Depersonalization* is a "this isn't me" feeling, as if the crime was happening to someone else. This can happen to small children who have been physically or sexually abused. Some of them have imagined they were someone else while attacked and developed a multiple personality disorder. *Derealization* is a "this isn't really happening" feeling as if you are in a dream or movie.

4. *Depression.* Victims of violent personal crimes report feeling trapped, defenseless, and in a hopeless situation. Mental imagery and energy have no place to go except down and in, as feelings of weakness, inadequacy, inferiority, and futility that easily combine and deepen if untreated into depression.

5. *Flashbacks.* Most victims have flashbacks, reliving the crime situation. This can occur whether the crime involved injury or loss with no contact whatever with the criminal. In some cases the crime recurs in slow motion during the day (usually at an idle or otherwise relaxing time) but most frequently in dreams. Sometimes dreams are of other equally unpleasant situations, symbolizing the original crime.

6. *Phobia.* Most crime victims are sensitized by the crime, conditioned by it to feel anxious or insecure in similar places or situations or with people who somehow resemble the assailant. A child who was ritually abused panicked in court when she saw the judge enter the courtroom in his black robes, similar to those used by cult members who abused her. This is a phobic reaction beyond normal, an exaggerated fear based on a previous painful event.

If a Loved One Is Killed

Grief over the sudden loss of a loved one can be mixed

with hate for the person or persons responsible. Both are natural, normal reactions to severe loss and the overwhelming stress of sudden, unexpected tragedy. Whether feelings of grief and loss occur alone or coupled with rage, these powerful emotions must be vented, channeled, and processed or they can affect physical and mental health. It is important to realize and accept the reality of the pain; do not deny it or refuse to do anything about it. As painful as it feels, it is important to know that it will lessen over time. You can recover and even grow from it. Most authorities estimate it takes up to a year and a half to process grief; much longer if it is denied or avoided. Without help or dealing with it, unresolved grief can last a lifetime.

Grief shows itself in many ways:

- anger and rage against the killer, witnesses who stood by, the police, the community, society in general, even God
- guilt that somehow, in some way, you could have anticipated the situation and done something to prevent it
- depression, emptiness, futility, or hopelessness because no one and nothing can ever "bring him/her back"
- low self-esteem: "I'm nothing without him/her"
- physical problems, mostly fatigue, lack of energy, feeling drained: "What's the use?"
- chronic irritability or restlessness, inability to concentrate on or finish a task, and alienating trusted friends ("How can you know how I feel?")
- alcohol or drug abuse

To process grief, realize and accept it and find appropriate ways to vent it. Don't fight it, let it flow. This includes anger as well as hurt. Sharing your feelings with a trusted friend, clergy, or therapist is the best way. Don't stop the crying spells even though you feel they'll never stop. If it embarrasses others, do it privately. Let your feelings flow—they will end in time. If they feel too powerful and overwhelming, get help from a licensed mental health professional.

It's better to consult a professional and be told you don't need therapy than to need it and not go. Take care of yourself. Some days will be harder than others. You have to eat, sleep, get up, dress, and go to work or school or attend to everyday tasks even though you don't feel up to it. Attend to any health problems. Much of what you feel may be due to stress, but if symptoms persist see your doctor. Some medication may help. Beware of excessive drinking—you're in a vulnerable state for addiction.

Keep active by making lists of what you have to do day to day. Set time limits for each task. Reward yourself when you meet deadlines. Concentrate on future goals and list them, such as job change, moving, new hobbies, or vacation. Force yourself if you must to participate in church, clubs, groups of interest to you, or volunteer work. Get exercise. Check out local night school courses—study something you've always wanted to learn. Attend local support groups. Build a new support system for yourself, better than you had before.

Gradually, over time, switch from the dark side of loss and emptiness, irritation, and anger, to the bright side of favorite foods and activities, pleasant getaways, shared times with good friends, and making new friends. Watch comedies on television and read books and articles that are humorous or inspirational. Go to church or temple—a different location than usual if you do not yet feel comfortable meeting old friends. It's social and supportive.

To help grieving people, be a good listener. Just being there is a great help. Do *not* try to persuade or convince them that life can be beautiful. That can only happen in time, not by instant conversation. Suggest shared activities you can do together. Help with everyday routine—otherwise they may just sit and withdraw into deeper depression. Be patient with those who avoid changing rooms or discarding clothing of the deceased. They need them initially and will want only a memento or two when grieving has run its course.

Post-Traumatic Stress Disorder

Post-traumatic stress disorder (PTSD) is an anxiety disorder that can result from severe stress. It is common among victims of violent crime, natural catastrophe, war, or a severe accident. You should be familiar with the symptoms and seek help or urge others to do so if you or they have this treatable condition. Here's the "official" description of it from the *Diagnostic and Statistical Manual of Mental Disorders* of the American Psychiatric Association:

1. Experiencing a "markedly distressing" traumatic event "outside the range of usual human experience," that is life-threatening to one or others or involves "sudden destruction of one's home or community."
2. One or more of the following:
   (a) recurrent, intrusive flashbacks of the trauma (for children, re-enacting it in play)
   (b) recurrent dreams of it
   (c) sudden déjà vu, feeling it is recurring
   (d) "intense psychological distress" in similar places or situations
3. Avoiding similar situations or "numbing," which was not present before the trauma; reflected in three or more of the following:
   (a) avoiding thoughts or feelings associated with the

trauma

(b) avoiding activities or situations reminiscent of the trauma

(c) blocking; inability to remember an important aspect of the event

(d) marked lack of interest in significant activities and skills

(e) feeling detached or distant from others

(f) restricted emotions such as inability to have or express love for others

(g) doomsday feeling of "foreshortened future"

4. Increased anxiety by two or more of the following:

(a) difficulty falling asleep or staying asleep

(b) irritability or angry outbursts

(c) difficulty concentrating

(d) constant hypervigilance (being "on edge")

(e) jumpiness; exaggerated responses

(f) physical reaction in similar situations or places such as shaking, sweating, heart pounding, rapid breathing, feeling faint or dizzy.

5. These symptoms persist a month or more.

It is not good for your mental or physical health to suffer indefinitely with this or any other continuing problem. This is especially true if the problem does not fade within a reasonable time. Psychotherapy with or without medication can speed recovery and restore you to your normal self.

Therapy

Most crime victims find that they can't talk with just anyone about their victimization. Few listeners know how to handle it, what to say, and what's best left unsaid. It can be anti-therapeutic for someone to innocently ask, "Well, why were you there?" Some listeners may tire of your bringing up the subject, as if to avoid the reality, due perhaps to their own hang-ups or fears. Even those close to you may not be able to help you in the way you need it.

Whatever you do, do not suffer in silence. Get help. Mental health professionals are the logical source of that help. Your needs fall exactly into their area of expertise. The treatment goal should be to restore you to pre-crime functioning and *not* to remake your personality. As treatment progresses, areas of self-improvement may become evident. You may want to work on them in therapy, by yourself, at some later date, or not at all. It's your mind and your life.

There are many systems of therapy and many treatment methods, but all grew from three basic theories: psychoanalysis, behaviorism, and humanism. Sigmund Freud was the founding father of psychoanalysis. It is a historical method, meaning that therapists avoid dwelling on the present except as signposts back to the past that formed your behavior. Instinct and insight are emphasized.

John Watson, Ivan Pavlov, and B. F. Skinner formed the behaviorist approach, which suggested that who you are is the result of what happened to you from conception to this moment. Learning, conditioning, current thinking, and behavior are emphasized.

Carl Rogers and Abraham Maslow are usually credited with founding the humanist movement, which suggests that people are more than products of instinct and learning, proven by the works of artists, composers, and great leaders throughout history. They emphasized caring, fellow feeling, and self-actualization.

What would all these guys say of Vincent Van Gogh? A psychoanalyst might say he put his lifelong maladjustment on canvas. A behaviorist might say he learned to be a good artist. The humanist might say his art showed his genius.

How does this help you find a therapist? If you have the time and money and want to use therapy as deep, intensive self-study, a psychoanalyst may be more appropriate. If you want a "quick fix" to control bad habits since your victimization, check with a behaviorist. If you're feeling there must be more to life and more to you as a person, talk to a humanist. These assessments are grossly oversimplified: some therapists use techniques from all three of these major movements. Some therapies don't seem to fit well in any one of the three.

Therapists

If you decide to go to a therapist and do not know of any, think first about the kind of person you would prefer: man or woman; same age, younger, older; same race or religion. Your choice is very important. If you are not comfortable with your therapist, treatment can take longer and be less effective. Don't feel guilty shopping for the best therapist for you or sharing with a therapist your concerns. A therapist who objects to your selection process or your reservations is not the kind of person you can really open up to and should be deleted from your list without guilt or obligation. Likewise, if you are seeing a therapist regularly and feel uncomfortable or dissatisfied, *say so*. To be therapy smart is to be articulate and assertive. Suggest treatment goals be revised, and if the problem continues ask for a referral to another therapist or find a replacement yourself. Use the termination or transfer as part of therapy, your recovery and your personal growth. It changes a negative into a positive.

There is a bewildering variety of mental health professionals doing therapy today. It's best to go only to a therapist licensed in your state. This means their training, experience, and credentials meet an established standard and any serious disciplinary actions are on record and accessible to you.

Here's a brief description of the mental health professions available to you:

Psychiatrists are medical doctors who specialize in human behavior and can prescribe medications. American Psychiatric Association, 1400 K Street NW, Washington, DC 20005 (202-682-6000).

Psychologists are Ph.D., Psy.D., or Ed.D. behavioral specialists trained in personality assessment and psychological testing, and individual and group therapy. There are some master's degree psychologists, but they are not licensable in most states at the independent practice level. American Psychological Association, 750 1st Street NE, Washington, DC 20002 (202-336-5500).

Social workers are MSW or LCSW master's level practitioners trained in the "systems" approach that emphasizes the effect of family and society on the individual rather than the person alone, the emphasis being in psychiatry and psychology. National Association of Social Workers, 750 1st Street NE, 7th floor, Washington, DC 20002 (1-800-638-8799).

Professional counselors are licensed in many states and credentials range from master's to doctoral degrees plus two or more years of supervised clinical experience. American Mental Health Counselors Association, 5999 Stevenson Lane, Alexandria, VA 22304 (1-800-545-2223).

Marriage and Family Therapists are licensed in most states and have a minimum of a master's degree and two years of supervised experience. They treat individuals, couples, and families with variations of systems theory. American Association for Marriage and Family Therapy, 1100 127th Street NW, 10th floor, Washington, DC 20036 (202-452-0109).

Nurse practitioners are registered nurses with additional training and supervised clinical experience in psychotherapy. Contact your state board of nursing for further information.

Pastoral counselors are rabbis, priests, or ministers who have additional training and supervised practice in individual and family therapy. Ask the clergy person you are considering if he or she is a member of the American Association for Pastoral Counseling (AAPC).

Hypnosis. Hypnosis is especially helpful in processing the aftermath of crime victimization. After achieving deep relaxation it is possible to relive the painful experience, vent it, relieve stress, and regain emotional controls. Because it involves treatment of psychological trauma it is best to go to a licensed mental health professional with postgraduate training and supervised experience in hypnosis and who is a member of one of two national associations: American Society for Clinical Hypnosis (ASCH), 2200 E. Devon #291, Des Plaines, IL 60018 (708-297-3317); Society for Clinical and Experimental Hypnosis (SCEH), 128-A Kings Park Drive, Liverpool, NY 13090 (315-652-7299). To be super safe, seek a board diplomate in hypnosis by American boards of medicine, psychology, or social work.

Biofeedback. An EMG (electromyograph) is painless, with three small "pasty" electrodes, and is used to teach self-relaxation or, in conjunction with self-hypnosis, to manage stress and to reduce anxiety. Association for Applied Psychophysiology and Biofeedback, 10200 West 44th Avenue #304, Wheatridge, CO 80033 (303-422-8436).

Don't be afraid of psychotherapy. Going to a therapist does not mean you're crazy. While you may have it all together as you read this, under severe stress (such as during and after a crime) you may be in a state of psychological shock. People in that state can be forgetful, with slowed reflexes; jumpy, with exaggerated startle response; or have disturbing flashbacks of the crime day or night in dreams. If disturbing thoughts or feelings persist, become worse, or interfere with everyday living, they should be treated by a licensed mental health professional as soon after the crime as possible.

Solution-Oriented Brief Therapy

This is one of the newest developments in therapy that you may find useful. It isolates and treats only the immediate problem and does not proceed further. It evolved from the humanist tradition, which believes people know deep inside what is best for them. One way to do this is with an intense focus on positives in everyday life, even the most insignificant. Other methods include composing a strengths list (e.g., family, hobbies, skills, interests, and past "goods"); acting as if problems were over, enjoying the feeling, making it a habit, and adopting it permanently; contemplating what would happen if you woke up and all your problems were solved—how would you know, who would notice? Therapists are coaches and mirrors; they help clients find the positives, apply them more and more to everyday living, and realize a more positive attitude toward life, themselves, and others.

Self-Care

In addition to the help available from licensed mental health professionals, and if the crime has not been so severe as to warrant therapy, a three-step self-care process can help you recover from a crime's psychological effects:

1. *Awareness.* Use "mental radar" to scan your own innermost thoughts and feelings, not to judge or analyze them, but to gain a simple, direct awareness of them, letting them flow of and by themselves, as if you were a passive observer, reporter, or scientist conducting an experiment.

2. *Experiment* with a variety of ways of coping with disturbing, unpleasant thoughts and feelings. Try something you

ordinarily do not do to relax or distract yourself. For example:

(a) *Meditation.* The awareness step can be used as a form of meditation. Passive reflection of what is happening moment to moment in your mind and body can actually relieve stress. Meditating on a flower, garden, or other restful scene, concentrating on minute details of texture, color, smell, and slow movement is another powerful stress reducer. Doing this works like a mental circuit breaker to protect you against negative thoughts and feelings.

(b) *Think positively.* There is a positive aspect to every situation. Surviving a violent crime is a hard lesson in the need to protect yourself in the future and to help others do so. Having your most valued possessions stolen can teach you to focus more on the quality of life than on material things. Life and happiness are more important than what has been lost. Practice evaluating everyday behavior and situations, choosing the positive and overlooking and minimizing negative aspects. Exert a conscious effort every day to see life as a dynamic interplay of good and evil, and move toward the good. Buddha's first Noble Truth was "every living thing knows pain," and his final Noble Truth was "it need not be so" and can be overcome by mental discipline toward positive thoughts and feelings.

(c) *Humor.* Humor offsets and helps overcome anxiety and breaks the chain of recurring unpleasant memories and feelings. It *is* better to laugh than to cry. Humor is the antidote to depression. Develop it by reading more humorous stories, watching television and movie comedies, and looking for some aspect of humor in everyday life.

(d) *Verbal exercise.* You can talk yourself out of dark moods by *positive self-talk.* Apply the ideas described here by talking to yourself silently or aloud as if you were your own best friend, always positively. A variation is to think of what the person you most admire—in history, myth, religion, or real life—would say to you in such situations.

(e) *Exercise.* Working out physically not only helps your body function better but vents anxiety and keeps you occupied. When you are idle and isolated there is more time for what Shakespeare termed "a brooding melancholy."

3. *Stress inoculation.* Use every incident of high anxiety to sharpen and shape your coping skills. Every time you feel tense and nervous, it can be another step forward in personal growth and better stress management, an immunization shot against anxiety and depression. Stress inoculation is like building a house brick by brick, a fortress against negative thoughts and feelings.

VICTIM SERVICES

Many states provide a variety of special services for crime victims. *Victim assistance programs* help victims cope with the consequences of crime. *Victim compensation* is money paid to victims from state funds for unreimbursed medical bills or lost income resulting from the crime. *Victim rights acts* guarantee crime victims these rights:

1. That you be informed of emergency services including medical care as needed.

2. To be given the name and phone number of the prosecuting attorney to inform you of victims rights and legal safeguards against threats or stalking by offenders or their friends and family.

3. In court, to be provided with a private waiting room or area protected from the defendant and his or her family, friends, and witnesses.

4. To be informed if, when, and where a criminal has been released or has escaped, and the name and phone number of a police contact who is responsible for communicating that information to you.

If your state does not offer these services you may want to help advocate them. Most victim assistance programs have organized group sessions in which you can meet with others who have been through a similar trauma and a trained professional who can help you work through it. Phone your local district attorney or the National Organization for Victim Assistance (NOVA) to locate community victim services. NOVA operates a 24-hour hotline staffed by trained mental health professionals at 1-202-232-6682. Its general number is 1-800-879-6682.

Victim Impact Laws

Many states have victim impact laws, which were enacted as a reaction to increased public concern that offenders have been accorded more rights and privileges. These laws ensure a victim's right to make written and oral statements reporting economic loss, physical or mental problems, and the effect of the crime on the victim and his or her family. Oral statements can be made at the sentencing hearing and later at the parole board when the offender is eligible for release.

USEFUL RESOURCES

American Psychiatric Association (1987). *Diagnostic and Statistical Manual of Mental Disorders (DSM-III)*. Washington, DC: Author.

MacHovec, F. J. (1981). "Hypnosis to Facilitate Recall in Psychogenic Amnesia and Fugue States: Treatment Variables." *American Journal of Clinical Hypnosis, 24,* 7-13.

MacHovec, F. J. (1984). "The Use of Hypnosis for Post-Traumatic Stress Disorder." *Emotional First Aid: A Journal of Crisis Intervention, 1,* 14-22.

MacHovec, F. J. (1987). *Expert Witness Survival Manual*
    Springfield, IL: Charles C. Thomas.
MacHovec, F. J. (1988). *Humor: Theories, History, and Ap-
    plications.* Springfield, IL: Charles C. Thomas.
MacHovec, F. J. (1989). *Interview and Interrogation: A
    Scientific Approach.* Springfield, IL: Charles C.
    Thomas.
MacHovec, F. J. (1990). *Private Investigation: Principles and
    Practice.* Springfield, IL: Charles C. Thomas.
Maslow, A. H. (1970). *Personality and Motivation.* New York:
    Harper and Row.
Walter, J. L., & Peller, J. E. (1992). *Becoming Solution-
    Oriented in Brief Therapy.* New York: Brunner/Mazel.

CHAPTER 6

Prevention

This book began with Murphy's Law, ("If anything can go wrong, it will") and Mac's Laws I and II ("If a crime can occur, it will," and "You can be a victim as easily as anyone else"). Anyone can be a crime victim at any time. You can be the right person in the wrong place at the wrong time. But as you've learned so far, most crime can be prevented if you take steps to prepare yourself in advance. Crime prevention is a matter of personal and public concern. It is personal because only you can take steps to ensure your survival. It is public because the cost of crime affects everyone, from neighborhood to nation.

Modern technology has given us advanced electronics that have reduced crime. Banks and stores have video scanning equipment to see and record any wrongdoing and loud or silent alarms to expose it. Electronics scan our luggage for weapons at airports, our bodies for shoplifted goods in stores, a suspected criminal's blood for a DNA match with that at the crime scene, and counterfeit money and forged checks. The sad truth is that technology is light years ahead of crime prevention.

To be effective, crime prevention must do more than be *reactive*—police responding and citizens defending themselves. Crime prevention must also be *proactive*, developing community awareness, citizen readiness to take an active part beyond self-protection, and services to high-risk potential criminals and convicted offenders. It's a three-pronged effort: *community programs*, from neighborhood to city, city to state; *personal security* of you, your loved ones, and property, including personal efforts at crime prevention; and *offender services*, to remove and rehabilitate criminals and identify and isolate persons at high risk of becoming criminals.

COMMUNITY PROGRAMS

The current widespread "conspiracy of silence" among witnesses reluctant to cooperate with police and victims who refuse to report crimes and press charges must stop. The police symbolize the highest values of society—law, order, and justice. Exceptions make the news, but the vast majority of criminal cases are handled well with due regard for the rights of victims and offenders. We need to develop a community spirit of shared values that considers any crime unacceptable behavior.

We need to focus more on similarities than dissimilarities. Pride in race, national origin, region and city, age, gender, or sexual preference can enrich the nation in a beautiful mosaic of fascinating differences. But our common impulses for a just and civil society should transcend these differences and unite us as a society. There was a time even in big cities when a youngster who did anything wrong arrived home to find his or her parents waiting and fully aware of the wrongdoing. Neighbors and family friends phoned ahead like a special crime telegraph line.

Today we are a society of transients separated from parents and birthplace, moving with jobs, hardly knowing our neighbors, too busy to join with them to develop a family feeling within the community. Evidence of this breakdown in society has been around since the industrial revolution a hundred years ago. German sociologists describe two major communities: *Gemeinschaft* (small town intimacy) and *Gesellschaft* (big city aloofness). In his book *The Lonely Crowd* David Riesman described anomie, the feeling of loneliness and depression even in families or groups with similar interests. In *Escape from Freedom* Erich Fromm reported how in Nazi Germany people followed Hitler because the alternative was an emptiness they could tolerate even less. Street gangs offer youth and adults alternatives to a lifestyle that is missing something.

We need to join together as one people, in fellow or community feeling to make the streets safe again. We need what the political analyst Walter Lippmann described as "a public conscience." As any day's news media shows, we're a very long way from it. Neither Democrat nor Republican presidents have had a plan or program to get us there. This is not surprising because it is a matter not of politics but of personal and community commitment, part of a basic belief system. It is "caught and not taught," so it won't happen overnight. As the Chinese philosopher Lao-Tse observed 2,500 years ago, "The journey of a thousand miles begins with the first step." Here are some steps we can take toward that goal:

1. *Every crime should be reported and every criminal prosecuted.* "If you do the crime, you do the time" should be the motto voiced throughout every community. It doesn't matter who you are—white, black, or purple—crime is 100

percent wrong and should be stopped. The quickest, most effective way to stop it is to report crime. If all crime were reported, the crime rate would eventually drop. It is a civic duty to report crimes. It is also a personal duty to protect yourself and your loved ones and do all you can to prevent crime.

2. *Eliminate high-crime environments.* Family dysfunction, lack of values, lack of education and money, mental and physical illness, alcohol and drug abuse, racism and sexism—these are the seedground of crime and violence. We must work harder to fulfill the American dream of one people that can agree to be different peacefully and without violence.

3. *Make more people street smart.* Do this through public awareness programs in the media, in schools, and in neighborhoods. People must wake up to crime, as you have by reading this book, like kids who regrettably must be taught to be wary of strangers. You can help increase crime awareness as a role model encouraging crime reporting or as a volunteer worker in crime prevention programs or rape crisis centers.

There are programs in every community that can and do prevent crime. There is DARE drug awareness, Job Corps, Police Athletic League (PAL), YMCA and YWCA programs, Boy Scout and Girl Scout merit badges on crime prevention, and Big Brothers and Big Sisters to name but a few. These organizations and programs can fight crime even more by training their members and officials to detect and deter sex offenders and refer them and substance abusers to get help.

Neighborhood Crime Watch. This is a nationwide movement of citizens like you who join together to help protect themselves and their property. They are the extra eyes and ears of police, Good Samaritans to each other. They operate with block captains and a phone network to alert the neighborhood to crime and suspicious persons in the area. If everyone participated in this worthwhile movement we would restore the friendship and cooperation of the old days. There would never be a riot or looting when neighbors insist on law and order and do not tolerate illegal activities by anyone.

Safe Streets is an FBI-sponsored program to deter street crime and interstate theft and include civilian patrols (Red Hat Coalition) and Adopt-a-School and Junior G-men crime prevention programs. For more information contact your nearest FBI field office or phone 202-324-4245.

Business Watch is a crime prevention program of local businesses that join together to protect stores and offices and the streets and parking lots in the area.

Police–Security Collaboration. Local police and security officers are joining together to form forums and councils to pool their resources to fight crime. In the State of Washington, local, state, and federal law enforcement representatives joined private security representatives in the Washington Law Enforcement Forum to monitor crime trends, network to control them, and operate a phone hotline for leads. In the Midwest, the Downtown Detroit Security Executives Council is a coalition of law enforcement and private security that has identified high-crime areas and coordinated police and security services there. In the east, police joined with security services in Baltimore County in a joint effort to prevent crime.

Citizen patrols are unpaid volunteers working closely with local police who patrol the neighborhood on foot or in their own pooled cars to report illegal or suspicious activities. They are not sworn police officers and do not apprehend suspects or participate in car chases. They observe and report. Property crime in Camden, New Jersey—once the second highest in the nation—dropped 41 percent after citizen patrols began. Why don't *you* participate in your local citizen patrol? If there isn't any, help organize one.

Auxiliary Police. Some cities and counties have auxiliary police or police reserves. They wear uniforms similar but not identical to local police, and in most areas they are unarmed.

They undergo a formal training program and are placed in areas of need, usually with regular police nearby. They function like the citizen patrols described above.

The Guardian Angels. These "red berets" were begun by Curtis Sliwa in New York City in 1979, patrolling subways for rapists and thieves. They are a multi-racial organization of men and women ranging in age from fifteen to the mid-twenties and wearing distinctive red berets and white T-shirts. They are trained in the martial arts and make citizens' arrests if needed. Critics consider them vigilantes, but many citizens feel they are well named: guardian angels.

Rape Crisis Centers provide immediate crisis intervention, temporary shelter if needed in "safe houses," referral for psychotherapy, advocacy and support at police interview and in court, support groups, and information on sexual abuse. At these centers there are professional therapists and former victims who volunteer to help others with a genuine interest in helping restore victims to well-being. Usually these centers include services for battered women and overlap with victims' services. These centers were founded by women as a sympathetic addendum to the criminal justice system.

Court Watchers. Some concerned citizens attend criminal court trials and track and report patterns of sentencing. Judges considered too lenient to offenders or too indifferent to victims are identified. Findings are made known regularly, especially at election time. Some groups also record judges' punctuality, workload, and courtroom demeanor.

CB radio. Many police departments monitor CB Channel 9, and in well-populated areas active CB networks provide a valuable link from citizens in their cars to police dispatchers. A mobile radio transmitter is helpful in reporting crime and accidents and also in tracking stolen cars or vehicles escaping crime scenes.

PERSONAL SECURITY AND CRIME PREVENTION

A personal security program is what you do for yourself to ensure your safety, the purpose and goal of this book. There are two parts: *personal*, protecting yourself and loved ones, and *property*, protecting your belongings.

The golden rule to prevent personal crime is: *Look out.* That includes hesitation before leaving safety to look out for any suspicious people or where they might be hiding, then proceeding on your way with "what if" readiness according to your pre-planned personal security system. It requires developing a "crook's-eye view" of targets of opportunity a criminal would see and remembering Mac's Law, that if a crime can happen, at some time it will. This does *not* mean being fearful or paranoid, but rather self-confident and cautious. It does not mean that because you think like a crook you feel like a crook.

The golden rule to prevent property crime is: *Lock up.* This includes routinely locking your car when you are in it and when you are not in it, the same for your home, office, and desk or cabinet drawers. Weapons should be locked away in concealed or inconspicuous places when you are not there. It may be inconvenient, but many illegal guns on the street have been stolen from places just like those *you* use. The tightest gun control laws won't stop thieves from breaking into your home and stealing your gun. Having to lock up guns and valuables does not mean you must feel like a captive or prisoner in your car, home, or office, or a hunted animal on the street. It does mean feeling as safe as possible wherever you are. Guidelines for crime prevention at the personal level follow.

1. *Check your security needs and vulnerability.* Having read this far, how safe do you feel you are on a scale of one to ten (ten being the safest)? Stated another way, what is your

overall rating of readiness to prevent and cope with crime? Where are you deficient? Make a list. Whatever you can imagine can happen might happen.

2. *Security actions.* What can you do now to reduce your risk of becoming a crime victim? Make a list of specific actions you agree to take. Don't forget that one of the best crime preventives is not being there but if you are, not being there alone. Think about where you go, when, and with whom. Minimize the risk factors. This does not mean you have to change your lifestyle or quality of life. It does mean that you must take action to preserve them and to ensure you will continue to enjoy them.

Here are fourteen personal crime prevention guidelines, seven unlucky don'ts and seven lucky do's:

Don'ts

1. **Don't** advertise yourself. Tell only a small circle of friends and relatives about trips or your daily schedule.

2. **Don't** leave notes on doors or mailbox.

3. **Don't** list your first name on the door, mailbox, or in the phone book.

4. **Don't** "dress rich" when in high-crime areas—it invites thieves.

5. **Don't** rely on chain locks on doors. They aren't worth a damn.

6. **Don't** go into elevators alone with a stranger or with one person in there unless you know them *well.*

7. **Don't** ever knowingly enter a danger area or, conversely, hesitate to leave a danger area.

Do's

1. **Do** pull down the shades and draw the curtains at

night.

2. **Do** install and use a peephole in the front door. Consider an intercom or black-and-white closed-circuit monitor. Both are small, easily concealed, and no longer expensive.

3. **Do** replace old locks and use solid cylinder deadbolts.

4. **Do** dress for easy running—no long coat or dress, tight pants, very high heels or platform shoes, or anything long and loose that could be used to drag you away or strangle or drag you.

5. **Do** use a buddy system whenever you can, especially when in unfamiliar places.

6. **Do** leave a light and radio on low when you are out. Leave some cash inside your home or office within easy view of the front door as you enter. Most thieves can't resist taking it. If it's missing as you open the door you will know someone's there or has been there *before you enter* and you can leave quickly and phone the police.

7. **Do** have emergency phone numbers at your fingertips wherever you are: in your purse and wallet, near the phone in kitchen and bedroom, on or at your desk at work, and in your car.

Psychic Signals?

Did you know you have a psychic crime prevention system? This sixth sense is part of your natural survival instinct. Chances are dogs and cats use this internal defense alarm more than you do. Observe and learn from them. It's being attentive to strange or unusual sounds, looks, and actions. Dogs and cats will often cant their heads to one side when this happens. But you don't have to see or hear anything suspicious to sense danger. It's been described as the feeling of hair standing up. Many feel it at the back of the neck. Some describe it as a feeling that someone's watching—there very well may be. Whenever you feel this tiny voice inside you saying, "Look out," don't take any chances. Walk toward safety, in full light, away from hiding places as fast as you can. It's better to be dead wrong than dead.

Visual Scanning and Recall

This is a useful crime preventive you can practice daily. Be more attentive to people and situations without staring or making others aware you're scanning. Minutes later remember all you can about them: clothing style and color, age, height, weight, hair, eyes, complexion, scars or tattoos, limps, rings and jewelry, unusual or distinguishing features. If you are ever a crime victim, your practiced visual scanning can make the difference between an unsolved crime and a crook behind bars.

OFFENDER SERVICES

In a free society, arrest, conviction, and sentencing are aimed at reformation and restitution. The only advantage to society when criminals just "do time" is their temporary absence from the street. The recidivism rate varies with the offense, burglary being the most frequently repeated crime (over 80%) and embezzlement the least repeated (less than 30%). Research shows that the recidivism rate drops when structured programs and therapy are provided to inmates during imprisonment. As we learn more about crime and criminals we can deter crime further, sentence more objectively, formulate treatment better, and refine rehabilitation programs.

Offender services can prevent crime by anticipating criminal behavior in high-risk individuals and reduce repeat offenses by providing rehabilitative services to offenders in community and residential corrections facilities. Fifty years ago Frank Tannenbaum wrote in his book *New Horizons in Criminology* that "good people" who try to rehabilitate criminals are "at the wrong end and too late." We need to identify personal and environmental factors that cause or encourage criminality and focus preventive services on them. This does not mean higher taxes and more programs. It can be included in existing child health care services, police training, and in schools and community agencies. Some of this is already happening, but more is needed.

While you may feel criminals should be denied rights and made to suffer for what they did, that is only part of the crime problem. If we did only that, prisons would be like holding cages for predatory animals to be released only when the timeclock for their offenses unlocked the cage door. The word *penitentiary* literally means "a place for penance." The current term is *correctional institution*, reflecting the change from punitive warehousing to rehabilitation. Today inmates can learn a trade and continue their education. Therapy specific to the crime is available. Sex offender treatment programs are an example. Victims volunteer as part of their therapy to participate in group sessions with offenders who committed similar crimes. Those sessions can be tearful and moving—with offenders doing the weeping. Inmates who become aware of the pain and suffering they inflicted are less likely to commit the same crimes again.

Diversion

Diversion is substituting community programs for prosecution or imprisonment. It's really informal probation, usually involves less serious offenses, and is designed to reduce court backlogs and prison overcrowding and to give offenders the opportunity to avoid a criminal record and remain in the community. Normal detention costs more than $50,000 per year for the average state prison inmate; diversion saves money and gives offenders a better chance to go straight.

Home detention or house arrest is a form of diversion in which offenders must remain home except for specified close-ly monitored times for work, medical care, shopping, or reli-gious services. Miniature transmitters worn on the ankle, wrist, or neck send a coded signal to a central computer and can detect movement 150 feet or more from the home loca-tion. One computer can monitor up to two thousand offenders.

Shock probation is another way we are trying to deter crime and at the same time alleviate prison overcrowding. Of-fenders are imprisoned for a short time to give them a taste of prison life, then spend the remainder of their sentences in the community.

Probation in jail is another variation, where offenders live in jail but leave to go to work or school.

Other Offender Services

Due process in prison. Since 1972 the U.S. Supreme Court has ruled that offenders have due process rights while in prison. For example, before a prisoner's good time credit is removed or reduced, or they are put in solitary confinement, prior written notice must be given and an impartial hearing held at which prisoners must be heard in person and allowed to present a defense.

Inmate councils. Some states allow prisoners to elect their own council to set and revise rules, a form of self-government.

Ombudsman. This is a state official usually appointed by the governor to receive and investigate complaints then re-port to the appropriate authority.

Civilian review boards. These boards hear complaints about police behavior and policies. They are composed of private citizens independent of the police department.

Pre-employment screening. Many firms today routinely do police checks. This is especially true if there are any government contracts involved.

Prisoners aid societies. Prisoners aid societies provide those with a prison record supportive services and help in finding jobs.

Community programs. There are a variety of support services available in the community, including street clinics that treat medical and mental problems, in-the-home family preservation programs, and residential programs such as supervised apartments, halfway houses, and clubhouse programs. Operating costs are paid for through local funds supplemented by grants and donations. There is access to specialized services such as psychiatric disorders, mental retardation, or substance abuse, usually through a case manager who knows local resources and makes referrals to them.

Youth services. Unless their crimes are very serious, juvenile offenders are charged and "adjudicated" (not "tried") in juvenile and family court, a less formal system than adult criminal court. This is the result of the "tender years" doctrine in Common Law that children are more easily rehabilitated and should be protected from hardened older criminals. In most states, the youth corrections department is also separate from adult corrections. Typically, the youth corrections department provides consultative services to courts, schools, and other state agencies, prepares statistical reports of its operations, and does self-research to improve its programs.

State mental health, mental retardation, and substance abuse services. These should collaborate with courts and corrections agencies in crime prevention programs for parents and the public. Mobile clinics have been helpful in providing individual, group, and family therapies to inmates and their families after release. This is especially helpful in rural areas when clients are far removed from clinic centers.

Government grants. These have funded residential and community sex offender and substance abuse treatment programs that have significantly reduced recidivism. As unemployment and immigration increase, similar programs and pilot projects in cultural diversity and anger control would further reduce hate crimes and riots.

"Son of Sam" laws. This type of legislation prevents convicted felons from making money by selling stories of their lives and exploits to movie or television producers and book or music publishers. In New York state, money from these sources is held in escrow for five years and is accessible to victims to finance civil suits for damages.

WHAT IS CRIMINALITY?

Crime prevention cannot be effective unless we know what criminality is, the risk factors to potential victims, and the types of persons most apt to become and remain criminals. We can become aware by reviewing crime statistics, case histories, and clinical research. Books by investigative reporters are especially helpful, such as Ann Rule's *Stranger Beside Me* about Ted Bundy. She knew him personally, having worked with him on a Seattle telephone crisis hotline. Even crime stories that are fiction and fantasy provide useful information, such as Robert Louis Stevenson's *Dr. Jekyll and Mr. Hyde*. As is true of most writers, his book was probably based on his own life experiences. Written in 1886, *Jekyll and Hyde* may be one of the world's first descriptions of multiple personality disorder.

From all these sources it is clear that crime is complex and has many causes. There are all kinds of crime and all kinds of criminals. We group crimes statistically, but many overlap and more than one can be committed at the same time, distorting the data. We group criminals by type, but many commit more than one kind of crime, making them difficult to understand. Sex offenders who peep, molest, and rape cross over non-violent and violent crime categories and non-contact and contact offenses. We classify and count criminals by age, sex, race, intelligence, and other physical factors, but important psychological factors are not yet included.

There are three areas that need immediate attention if we are to deal effectively with the growing crime problem.

1. *Early detection, prompt intervention.* An important aspect of crime prevention is to stop it before it gets out of hand. If people reported drug dealers every time they saw one in action, drug crime would be much less of a problem today. Youth who commit crimes should be sentenced *according to the crime*—not plea bargained to a lesser crime—so the problem behavior is clearly known for the record. This helps therapists and corrections specialists focus on treatment needs and quickly identify repeaters for more stringent controls.

2. *More data.* We need more accurate information as to biological, environmental, and psychological factors of offenders, types of crime and their frequency, victim choice, trigger situations, criminals' fantasies and personality dynamics. With this database we can develop training programs for parents, pediatricians, clergy, and teachers to identify traits and factors of high-risk form criminality. There is no early detection program for criminal psychopaths, yet we know that most show early signs of their killer instinct. To do nothing to detect and control it in early childhood is unconscionable.

3. *Better rehabilitation programs.* Somehow we must develop treatment methods fitted to specific crimes and

criminals' personalities. We especially need some way to foster societal values. Carnes recommends the Twelve-Step system of Alcoholics Anonymous, a non-denominational way of encouraging trust in a higher power outside oneself.

THE NATURE OF EVIL

There is no doubt that evil exists and crime is good evidence of that. There is no good or redeeming virtue in sadistic rapists or serial killers. To prevent crime we must first understand it. We cannot understand crime without understanding evil, where it comes from, and what it is. Many see evil as the work of the devil, a bad angel God threw out of Heaven who's behind all wrongdoing. Some believe that evil is simply the absence of good. Others see evil as a destructive force, the dark side of human nature.

Evil has existed throughout history, and it has not changed much over time and through different cultures. This suggests that times change but people do not. Was there a "Nazi mind" during World War II? Many people think so. It would be convenient to think that a certain kind of "nut case" or "arch criminal" could be responsible for genocide, torture, and protracted war in the face of massive losses and imminent defeat. Extensive personality testing was done to eight leading Nazi war criminals after World War II. In 1989, psychologists used the latest scoring systems to re-evaluate the data. They found *no* distinctive "Nazi mind." They found a variety of personality dynamics, from poor impulse control to severe thought disorder. We would probably get similar test data from a random sampling in any prison, probably on any street. To prevent crime we must be aware that good and evil exist everywhere, and we must develop programs specific to criminals and their crimes.

PSYCHOPATHY

There are degrees of severity and seriousness in evil and in crime. Getting a speeding ticket makes you an offender, but it is a minor violation. There is little or no evil intent. *Criminal psychopaths* may be the most evil people the world has ever seen. To be street smart you should know about them, if for no other reason than to avoid them in your daily life. As a society we must be able to detect and monitor them if they have not been arrested, and to develop intensive treatment programs to stop their destructive behavior. Many mental health professionals consider pure, classic psychopathy to be untreatable.

Psychopaths can be male or female, above or below average in intelligence, young or old, rich or poor, from good homes or dysfunctional families, and any race, religion, or national origin. They have never "bonded" with anyone or anything, animal or human. Behavior problems began at an early age, frequently with fire setting and animal torture. Charming at first, they are unable to maintain close long-term relationships. Good actors or actresses, they are able to fake emotion, but there's a plastic, artificial quality to it because they really have no empathy. They don't keep friends or jobs, have no realistic long-term goals, and usually lead a nomadic lifestyle, moving frequently or living off others until rejected. They also sleep around with many partners, no relationship lasting very long. They are really *un*socialized, as if strangers from an uncivilized land.

Psychopaths are basically extremely selfish; everything they do is for their own personal gain. They have an inflated self-concept, a grandiose self-worth. Impulsive and thrill-seeking, they commit a variety of crimes for a "high." They have no values other than self, no conscience, and therefore no guilt for anything they do. They are superb con artists, clever manipulators, and pathological liars. There is much talk but little action. If caught in a lie, they shrug it off as if it were a grammatical error. Theirs is a stainless steel personality, cold despite superficial charm. As criminals they are lethal loners like the gunfighters of the Old West, with the killer instinct and reflexes of predatory animals waiting to strike. Anthony Hopkins's portrayal of a psychopath in the movie *Silence of the Lambs* is an example. We appear *abnormal* to them, nothing more than targets for their own amusement, after which they can return home for a pleasant meal and restful, uninterrupted sleep.

It is important to put psychopathy in the correct context. There are degrees of psychopathy. You will see psychopathic traits or tendencies in people trying to sell you something—products, services, politics, or religion. You may notice a trace of it in family and friends, maybe even in yourself. Have you ever wondered about pillars of the community—doctors, lawyers, clergy, therapists, business and government leaders—convicted of serious crimes? Not all psychopaths are in prison. Psychopathy is a continuum, from occasional selfish thoughtlessness to vicious repeated violence and murder. Is psychopathy preventable? We don't know yet. For now, all we can do is exert every effort to stop it. We must recognize it, research its causes, develop effective treatment for it, and closely monitor for recidivism.

VALUES

The counterweight to evil is *good*. If everyone believed in good and shared the same value system, there would be no crime. We would also not need any police officers. It is, of course, the ideal; the world has never achieved a state of such virtue. Ironically, law, religion, and philosophy from ancient to modern times have been clear and consistent about good and evil, right and wrong. The golden rule is a teaching common to them all: Do unto others what you would have them do unto you.

One of the criteria used by parole boards, probation officers, and forensic experts when evaluating the mental state of suspects and criminals is the ability to know right from wrong and to conform to societal values—stated another way, to know the consequences of a criminal act. *Mens rea* (Latin for "guilty mind") is a legal term for a mind with evil intent. *Mala in se* is an act of and by itself that is morally wrong, an offense against conscience. Throughout the justice system there is an emphasis on values, what society considers to be good for the individual and the community. The problem is it is all *descriptive,* not *prescriptive.* The law does not tell us how to instill values in offenders. The mental health professions avoid it as more religious or philosophical than behavioral.

Because treatment of criminals does not completely eliminate recidivism, self-therapy and self-help groups are recommended based on guidelines similar to Alcoholics Anonymous. The primary focus is on character building and a non-religious yet spiritual personal values system, which in time and with practice replace impulsivity and the criminal mind. It's worth considering because there are now numerous "Anonymous" groups for a variety of excessive or habituated behaviors such as Debtors, Gamblers, Narcotics, Smokers, Overeaters, Bulimics, Anorexics, Sex Addicts, Child Abusers, Sexaholics, Incest Survivors, Shoplifters, Workaholics, Emotions, and Parents. Here are the Twelve Steps of AA adapted to control criminal behavior:

Twelve Steps to Criminal Rehabilitation

1. *Admit* there is a problem that has been and is beyond control.

2. *Need* for a higher power, outside and beyond yourself, to control it, change, and prevent re-offending. This higher power can be a real or imagined role model, in religion, history, literature, or current events and need not be God or a religious figure.

3. *Firm decision* and contract to be open to whatever is needed to change for the better.

4. *Self-inventory* of yourself, candid and detailed.

5. *Freely admitting* wrongdoing and weakness, past and present, whenever and wherever it occurs.

6. *Open, receptive, and appreciative* of therapy and help.

7. *Active search* for truth to overcome weakness.

8. *List* all who have been harmed, directly and indirectly, and be willing to make amends if possible and appropriate.

9. *Make amends* unless doing so is harmful in any way. Offer a genuine apology and do not ask for forgiveness to wipe the slate clean as if it didn't happen.

10. *Continued personal growth,* correcting errors as they become obvious or are made known to you.

11. *Continue to rely on and trust in a higher power* for good to phase out evil impulses and wrongdoing.

12. *Pass it on.* Help others do the same.

Using such a checklist of objectives broadens the scope of therapy and offers a solid value system to reinforce character development not presently part of traditional treatment. Eastern philosophies such as Buddhism, Taoism, and Zen offer simple techniques for positive character development that are easily understood and non-denominational. Buddha's Four Noble Truths and Eightfold Path address the same basic ideas as the Twelve-Step AA program.

● ● ●

The Four Noble Truths

Buddha's First Noble Truth is "the wheel," realization that to live is to know pain, that wherever there is life there are problems and conflict. Evidence includes birth, hunger, thirst, pain, injury, disease, aging, and death. Psychological aspects include anger, hate, fear, frustration, dissatisfaction, separation, aversion, and unpleasantness. Buddha taught that pleasure brings pain because we feel deprived or frustrated when we cannot have it.

The Second Noble Truth is "the wheel's hub," that much pain is self-inflicted, exaggerated by frustrated wants and needs, illusion, and materialism. A major negative aspect is ignorance, which Buddha described as darkness. The First and Second Noble Truths are pessimistic, looking at the dark side of human nature, the *yin* half of the yin-yang symbol of Taoism.

The Third Noble Truth is "the promise" that the pain need not be so. This step offers hope and enlightenment.

The Fourth Noble Truth is "the way"—the Eightfold Path. It is also known as "the middle way" or "message from the heart." The last two Noble Truths bring light to darkness, the *yang* force in the yin-yang symbol, completing the dynamics of everyday life. Transforming negative to positive is a basic principle of Buddhist psychology especially appropriate for rehabilitating criminals.

The Eightfold Path

The Eightfold Path is the treatment plan, interrelated steps Buddha described as interwoven strands of a rope ladder tied to the enlightened self. They are co-existent, need not be achieved in order like the Twelve Steps of AA, and they merge into a self greater than the sum of its parts. They are:

1. *Attitude (right view)* is a basic positive orientation to life based on understanding of self and others, truth and evil, their roots, the realities of suffering in thought and feeling, peace, and the Eightfold Path. Buddha taught that no single factor is as responsible for suffering as a wrong view, none as powerful in promoting good as a right view.

2. *Intent-motive (right wisdom)* is direction, purpose, or intent by self-control, free of negative influences such as selfishness, anger, hate, rudeness, or cruelty. This purity is achieved in three ways: by renouncing and avoiding sources of suffering by understanding them; by developing and applying caring and compassion to all; and by doing no harm.

3. *Speech-silence (right speech)* is stating truth simply or in silence, free of lies, gossip, or exaggeration; simplifying and unifying and not complicating or dividing. Wrongful speech is rooted in anger and hurts, makes enemies, and causes bitterness. Good speech is rooted in caring, and it heals, makes friends, and enhances wisdom. It is saying the right thing at the right time in the right way.

4. *Action-reaction (right action)* is letting every action weaken a fault or evil intent, to love life in all its forms without craving, excess, stealing, or killing. There are three wrong actions: killing or mistreatment; stealing; and wrongful sex. The counterbalance to killing is compassion; that for stealing is respect and generosity; and that for wrongful sex is love and mutual respect between equals.

5. *Livelihood (right livelihood)* is to revive and restore yourself. This means to realize that life is a mission and not just a career, that living is giving, that you keep only what you give away, and that every day is a challenge and opportunity to be lived as the last because some day it will be. Wrong livelihood is pursuit of power or profit by wrongdoing, directly or indirectly, or in an illegal, unethical, or harmful

occupation. It is better to cooperate than compete, to give than to take, and to render service to others without deception or misrepresentation.

6. *Attention (right effort)* is to be involved in whatever you're doing, wherever you are, and continue to develop your mind. There are seven factors: mindful insight; study of consequences; enthusiastic energy; reverie and rapture; tranquil contemplation; one-pointed concentration; and stimulus and response are seen equally well.

7. *Contemplation (right mindfulness)* is meditative awareness, "seeing with the third eye" and "hearing with the third ear" with open, unbiased sensitivity, impartial objectivity, serene detachment, and without any interpretation. The mind is in repose, quiet, unhurried, reflecting on function and not fiction. Objects of contemplation include the body, sensation, the mind, and inner thoughts and feelings.

8. *Concentration (right concentration)* or one-pointed mind is to realize a higher or cosmic consciousness from working at the Eightfold Path. Attention is focused on an object to settle or quiet the mind which is then purified, free of external and internal influences and no longer deluded or distracted. This step can be achieved from two directions: the "serenity path" as an end in itself; and the "insight path," achieved indirectly by working on and achieving the Eightfold Path.

The Twelve Steps of Alcoholics Anonymous and Buddha's Four Truths and Eightfold Path offer a values system and an organized system of character development missing in traditional corrections and therapy. The AA Twelve-Step program has been successful with thousands of substance abusers. Buddha's method has been followed by millions of people for centuries. Both can be used by anyone, without a therapist. No present system of therapy can match that record. Both fill in the gaps missing in current treatment. They can supplement current treatment models and would not in any way interfere with them.

MEDIA VIOLENCE

Movies and television dramas are popular diversions, and their content impresses and influences us. Some critics feel they have replaced the school and church in their power to gain our attention and condition us. There would be no commercials if viewers did not buy the advertised products. It is difficult to imagine that repeated portrayals of violence would not have some effect on the audience. It is estimated that by the time children complete elementary school they have seen 8,000 murders and 100,000 acts of violence in the visual media.

For centuries children have been exposed to violence in ghost stories and fairy tales. Today's horror, science fiction, western, and crime movies offer an even greater variety of scary stories. These productions cause disturbed sleep and nightmares. Defenders justify violence in cartoons because they are fantasy, not real; so are fairy tales. Some argue there is violence in popular music lyrics, from "Mac the Knife" to today's big hits. That is so, evidence we are engulfed in a media explosion that contains the sights and sounds of violence. Violence in television news coverage is controlled only by the news editor and program director. Violent acts and themes in music, movies, and television stories are controlled by the ratings, the market, not by concern for morality or potential negative psychological effects on viewers.

Whether violence in movies, television, and music glamorizes crime and potentiates violence continues to be a raging controversy between a concerned public and media management. It has been debated in Congress for decades. In 1993 the four major television networks, ABC, CBS, NBC, and Fox, began running parental advisories before and during programs that contained violent acts. These advisories assume there is a parent present and aware of this method for limiting children's exposure to violence. Advisories may be an attractive nuisance, arousing curiosity and motivating children to watch anyway. It was a unified effort of the television industry to police itself rather than risk the increasing the probability that Congress would enact restrictive legislation limiting media violence. Cartoons, news telecasts, cablevision, and networks other than the "big four" were not included in the industry screening system.

Rising public and congressional concern and the industry response to it are evidence of a perceived and acknowledged problem. Still controversial and an area in need of more data, research studies are beginning to show a correlation between media and real-life violence. We need more careful research before we can come to a definitive conclusion. It might help to have an index of violent acts per hour as part of a rating system in addition to parental advisories. If we find that there is a correlation between television and real-life violence, industry self-monitoring and government regulation should set firm and reasonable limits in the public interest.

USEFUL RESOURCES

Carnes, P. (1989). *Contrary to Love: Helping the Sexual Addict.* Minneapolis, MN: CompCare Publishers.

Fromm, E. (1941). *Escape from Freedom.* New York: Rinehart.

Hickey, E. W. (1991). *Serial Murderers and Their Victims.* Pacific Grove, CA: Brooks/Cole.

MacHovec, F. J. (1989). *Cults and Personality.* Springfield, IL: Charles C. Thomas.

Meloy, J. R. (1988). *The Psychopathic Mind: Origins, Dynamics, and Treatment.* Northvale, NJ: Jason Aronson.

Meloy, J. R. (1992). *Violent Attachments.* Northvale, NJ: Jason Aronson.

Ressler, R. K., Burgess, A. W., & Douglas, J. E. (1988). *Sexual Homicide: Patterns and Motives.* Lexington, MA: Lexington Books.

Riesman, D. (1950). *The Lonely Crowd.* New Haven, CT: Yale University Press.

Robin, G. D., & Anson, R. H. (1990). *Introduction to the Criminal Justice System.* 4th edition. New York: Harper & Row.

Rule, A. (1980). *The Stranger Beside Me.* New York: New American Library.

Epilogue

Until now, most books on personal security have recommended passive surrender to save your life. That's still good advice, but times are changing. There are senseless killings of victims who do not resist, or who just happen to be on the crime scene. In a Maryland carjacking, a mother reached for her infant daughter, caught her arm in the car door, and was dragged two miles to her death. In Texas a deluded gunman drove his truck into a restaurant then randomly shot the people there. In California a man armed with three guns got off the elevator on the thirty-fourth floor of a skyscraper office building, killing eight and wounding many more. In New York terrorists attempted to blow up the World Trade Center, killing six and injuring more than a thousand. The bottom line is: *You could have been in any of those places.* If you had been, what would you have done? If you had had the means to fight back, would you have? It's a judgment call and one that only you can make. Don't delay. Tomorrow *you* may be in a situation similar to those just described.

Crime will not stop by itself. It has never run out of steam. If you do nothing, it will continue. There will be many more victims. It is better to light one candle than to curse the darkness; crime thrives in darkness. As more candles are lit, criminals will slink away into the shadows. As Voltaire so wisely observed centuries ago, "No army can withstand the force of an idea whose time has come." *Now* is the time to take a hard look at crime and what you personally can do about it. Truly, the life you save may be your own or your loved one's.

If you find this book helpful, recommend it to others to help them become street smart. If you feel safer and more self-confident after reading it and more secure putting its suggestions into effect in your daily life, the goal of this book has been achieved. As you and others read it and improve your personal security, the streets will be safer and the crime rate reduced. It's an old teaching that whatever good you have found should be passed on.

And if you've been an unlucky victim of crime and have to pick yourself up and work through the psychological and physical hurt, may the "old philosopher's credo" help you along the road to recovery. If you can say it and realize it month to month, year to year, you will know the ugly past is fading. It is with this sincere message to you that this book ends:

I ain't what I wanna be
I ain't what I'm gonna be
But I sure as hell
Ain't what I used to be

May it always be so for you.

Resources

Adult Protective Services, or Women's Shelter or Rape Crisis Center. Call local police to locate these community services to report spouse abuse.

American Association of Retired Persons (AARP), Program Department, 1909 K Street NW, Washington, DC 20049. Sponsors local groups of widowed persons and other services.

Aviation Crime Prevention Instiutute, P.O. Box 3443, Frederick, MD 21701 (301-694-5444).

Child Protective Services. Call local police to locate this community social service agency to report child physical, sexual, or ritual abuse.

Crime Watch, Crimestoppers, Neighborhood Watch, Business Watch. Contact your local police or sheriff for more information.

Drugs and Crime Data Clearinghouse, 1600 Research Blvd.,

Rockville, MD 20850 (800-666-3332).

Federal Bureau of Investigation, J. Edgar Hoover Building, Washington, DC 20535. Call 202-324-3000 for the nearest FBI field office, with 24-hour phone service. The FBI sponsors the Safe Streets, Red Hat Coalition, Adopt-a-School, and Junior G-men programs.

International Association of Campus Law Enforcement, 638 Prospect Avenue, Hartford, CT (203-233-4531).

International Association of Credit Card Investigators, 1620 Grant Avenue, Novato, CA 94947 (415-897-8800).

International Association for Hospital Security, P.O. Box 637, Lombard, IL 60148 (312-953-0990).

International Association for Shopping Center Security, 2830 Clearview Place NE, Suite 300, Atlanta, GA 30340 (404-457-3575).

Justice Department Clearinghouse, Box 6000, Rockville, MD 20850 (301-251-5500; computer BBS: 301-738-8895).

Juvenile Justice and Delinquency Prevention, 633 Indiana Avenue NW, Washington, DC 20531 (202-307-0751). Juvenile Justice Clearinghouse 800-638-8736.

National Victims Resource Center (800-627-6872). Victim services.

National Institute of Justice, Box 6000, Rockville, MD 20850 (800-851-3420). Publications, videotapes, bibliographies.

National Computer Security Association, 4401-A Connecticut Avenue NW, Suite 309, Washington, DC 10008 (717-258-1816).

National Crime Prevention Council, 1700 K Street NW, 2nd floor, Washington, DC 20006-3817 (202-466-6272). Crime dog "McGruff" program, publications, resource center, computer database.

National Retail Merchants Association, 100 W. 31st Street,

New York, NY 10001 (212-244-8780). Crime and loss prevention programs for retail businesses.

Office of Hazardous Materials Transportation, U.S. Department of Transportation, Washington, DC 20590 (information 202-887-1255; emergencies only 1-800-424-9900). This federal agency publishes an emergency response guidebook.

Pro-Tech Inc., P.O. Box 3658, Richmond, VA 23227 (804-358-6005). Reliable information on personal security devices.

U.S. Department of Justice, Office of Juvenile Justice and Delinquency Prevention. Call 202-307-0598 to report missing children.

Index

INDEX

Minors (*see* Juvenile offenders)
Miranda rights, 119
Money, as crime motive, 26
Motor vehicle theft (*see also* Carjacking), 13, 15
Moving and maneuvering car, 76-77
Murder, 10-11
Murphy's Law, 1, 145
Mutilation, 27

National Organization for Victim Assistance (NOVA), 143
Necessity defense, 123
Negligence, legal test for, 124
Neighborhood Crime Watch program, 148
News media, dealing with, 115-17
Nolle or *nol pros*, 121
Nolo contendere, 121
Numbing effect of trauma, 135
Nurse practitioners, 139

Objectivity, need for, 18
Obstructing justice, 13
Offender services, 154-55
Office crime, 15, 83-98
Ombudsman, 156
Opening statement, in court, 121
Opioids (*see* Drugs)
Orientation, 18
Overcharging to prosecute, 121

Paranoid erotomania, 56-57
Paranoid feelings, 17
Parking lot crime, 15, 104
Parole/probation, 123, 155-56
Pastoral counselors, 139
PCP (*see* Drugs)
Pedophiles (*see* Child molesters)
Personal and household crime, 13

Personal security, 2, 151-53
Personality testing, 160
Phobia, from crime, 131
Pimping, 13
Poachers, 108-9
Police investigation, 114-15
Police imposters, 4, 66-68, 72
Police response to crime, 16
Police-security collaboration, 149
Pornography, 13, 27
Post office shootings, 85
Post-traumatic stress disorder (PTSD), 134-35
Power, as crime motive, 26
Preponderance of evidence, 121
Priest imposters, 4
Professional counselors, 138
Profiles: criminal, 7-8, 10-11, 25-29, 32, 57-59, 85-86, 89-90, 161-62; victim, 11, 15-16, 25, 85-86, 90-91, 99-100
Proof, legal, 121
Property crime, 12-14; security, 151-53
Prostitution, 13
Psychiatrists, 138
Psychic danger signals, 153-54
Psychoanalytic therapy, 136-37
Psychological hooks, 79-80
Psychological effects of crime, 130-33
Psychologists, 138
Psychopathy, 161-62
Public places, crime in, 15
Public conscience, need for, 147
Punishment, vs. rehabilitation, 155, 159-60
Punitive damages, 124

Rape crisis centers, 151
Rape, 3, 11-12, 13, 15, 113-14

INDEX

ABOUT THE AUTHOR

Frank MacHovec is a licensed private investigator and licensed clinical psychologist with twenty-five years of experience in mental health and security services. He has authored several books and numerous journal articles and regularly speaks at local, state, and national security and mental health services conferences. He is a Fellow and Diplomate of the American Board of Medical Psychotherapy, Adjunct Associate Professor of Psychiatry and Behavioral Medicine at the University of Virginia, and past President of the Virginia Association for Marriage and Family Therapy.